SLAM

THE

DOOR

GENTLY

Slam the Door Gently

THE MAKING AND UNMAKING OF A FEMALE SCIENTIST

Ruth Ann Bobrov Glater, Ph.D.

FITHIAN PRESS

SANTA BARBARA, 1997

The quoted passage on page 180 is from *Fair Science: Women in the Scientific Community* by Jonathan R. Cole, copyright © 1987 by the Columbia University Press. Reprinted with the permission of the publisher.

The prayer on page 212 is reprinted from Greenberg, Moshe; Greenfield, Jona; and Sarna, Nahum; *The Book of Job, a New Translation* (New York: Jewish Publication Society, 1980), Verse 42, p. 62.

The lyrics on page 229 are from *The Colors of My Life* by Cy Coleman and Michael Stewart © 1980 Notable Music Co., Inc. All rights administered by WB Music Corp. All rights reserved. Used by permission. Warner Bros. Publications U.S., Inc., Miami, FL 33014.

The invocation on page 232 is adapted from Rokeach, David, *Gates of Repentence: The New Union Prayerbook for the Days of Awe* (New York: Central Conference of American Rabbis, 5738–1978).

Published by Fithian Press
A division of Daniel and Daniel, Publishers, Inc.
Post Office Box 1525
Santa Barbara, CA 93102

Design by Eric Larson

LIBRARY OF CONGRESS CATALOGING-IN-PUBLICATION DATA
Glater, Ruth Ann Bobrov, (date)
    Slam the door gently : the making and unmaking of a female scientist / Ruth Ann Bobrov Glater.
        p.   cm.
    ISBN 1-56474-187-7 (pbk. : alk. paper)
    1. Glater, Ruth Ann Bobrov (date). 2. Woman botanists—United States—Biography. 3. Botanists—United States—Biography.
    I. Title
QK31.G58A3   1997
581'.092—dc20
    [B]   96-19361
                                          CIP

*To Armando Quiros,
who has made all the difference*

CONTENTS

A section of photographs begins on page 145

FOREWORD

At last the exhilarating, poignant, and ultimately shocking story of the great physicist Lise Meitner has been fully and vividly told. Deprived of the Nobel Prize she so clearly deserved for her contribution to the discovery of nuclear fission, Lise Meitner has never been given the attention she deserves in the history of twentieth-century physics. Now, with grace, style, and great authority, [author] Ruth Sime sets the record straight.

So begins the description of a new biography published in 1996 by the University of California Press.

The stories of Lise Meitner, an internationally renowned physicist and mathematician, and Ruth Ann Bobrov Glater, a marginally employed botanist in the UCLA School of Engineering, seem at first glance to have little in common. Separated by generation, reputation, and the Atlantic Ocean, the two nonetheless shared certain commonalities. Both were women, both Jews, both scientists. Each braved the sexism of the scientific world and each found in that world professional betrayal. When the rise of Nazism forced Meitner to flee Germany, her male collaborator took full credit—and the 1944 Nobel Prize—for the work they had done jointly on nuclear fission. When Glater finished her Ph.D., her fellow botanists praised her work, published her research in academic journals, yet denied her a place in the academy.

While Meitner's story found a biographer, Glater's predictably did not. Convinced that she had a story to tell, Glater produced her own manuscript and submitted it to major presses. Her account, she was informed, was indeed well written and very moving, but only the autobiographies of well-known individuals sell. Projected sales figures did not appear to justify publication. Those who believe they know Ruth Glater well as well as those to whom her name is unfamiliar are the beneficiaries.

Slam the Door Gently is, as its subtitle suggests, an account of the making and unmaking of a female scientist. Set in an era before sex-based discrimination in education and employment became a problem to be redressed through public policy, Glater's struggle to enter and to advance in the overwhelmingly male-dominated scientific establishment was shared by women in other professions. But while law, medicine, and certain areas of academia slowly incorporated larger numbers of women during the 1970s and '80s, the sciences proved especially resistant. By 1987, two decades after the feminist movement began, only sixteen percent of the employed scientists and engineers in this country were female. The imbalance has shifted in some fields more than others— forty-one percent of working biologists and life scientists are now women, whereas only one percent of working environmental scientists are female. Yet irrespective of their field, women scientists typically earn salaries that are about twenty-five percent lower than those paid to men in the same positions. They are twice as likely to be unemployed, and they are rarely promoted to the highest positions. In 1993, the most recent year for which figures are available, women held barely ten percent of the full professorships in the sciences and engineering in the nation's universities and colleges and only twenty-one percent of the associate professorships.

Statistics are limited in what they reveal. Equally impersonal are the surveys that document contributing factors such as fewer role models, less mentoring, greater isolation, and harassment that young women in the sciences experience. Glater's autobiography personalizes these statistics, revealing the extraordinary psychological costs that such discrimination exacted on the individuals who experienced it. The pain is still palpable. Nor was there an analgesic in the form of an alternative career such as that found by the accomplished British mycologist Beatrix Potter. Denied membership in professional societies because of her sex despite her scientific discoveries, Potter turned to writing and illustrating children's books, to the delight of generations of English-speaking children and their parents. Yet *Slam the Door Gently* is ultimately not a story of male villainy or female victimization. Rather it is about struggle in the face of problems that were personal as well as professional, self-inflicted as well as externally imposed.

Resilience was part of Glater's heritage as a Jew. Her family was one of the many that made the transition from the tiny towns of eastern Europe, *shtetlach* as they were called, to the suburbs of the United States. Born into the world of *Yiddishkeit*, a traditional culture in which Yiddish was the everyday language of the masses, religion dominated every aspect of life, and family formed the bedrock of Jewish identity. Glater's parents were part of one of the greatest migrations in history. Of the millions of Jews who fled the virulent anti-Semitism and pogroms of czarist Russia, nearly two million had settled in New York City alone by the outbreak of World War I.

Clustered initially in the lower east side of the city, some of these new arrivals later made their way to the Brownsville area of Brooklyn and to the Bronx in an effort to escape the noise and congestion of the east side. Visiting the Bronx in 1903, a Yiddish journalist described it as a beautiful area with space, clean air, and sunshine. But landlords, he noted, were quickly erecting tenements. The Bronx, he predicted, was becoming "our new ghetto." His prediction proved correct—at least for some neighborhoods. Nine years later, a visiting English novelist would describe the east Bronx as a harsh environment "to which the fit will be attracted, and where the fit will survive." It was in a small, dark room in a Bronx tenement two stories above her father's kosher butcher shop that Ruth Bobrov was born.

Her father, Jacob Bobrov, who had arrived from Russia in 1904, was a *schochet*, one who performed the ritual slaughtering of meat that rendered it kosher—acceptable for eating by Orthodox Jews. His trade as a butcher enabled him to observe the Sabbath, his first priority. Orphaned at the age of two, he had spent his days in the *yeshiva* where the men of the small *shtetl* of Berisiv met to study and discuss the Torah and Talmud, turning in the evenings to charitable villagers for food and lodging. As was true of many deeply religious Orthodox men from the old world, his heart was in study, not the shop. Denied the status that their learning had entitled them to in eastern Europe, such men were ill prepared to cope with the economic pressures of life in the United States. It was their wives who were compelled to handle the business of daily living. The Bobrovs were no exception. It was the energetic, resourceful Jennie Bobrov who assumed responsibility for making ends meet, working in the shop long hours alongside her husband to ensure that there was food for her own table.

For the young Ruthie, there was growing up to do—a daunting experience in the inhospitable environment of the east Bronx in a family richer in morals and energy than material possessions or psychological insight. Glater's account of the early years vividly evoked a world familiar to many immigrant children: the noise of elevator trains rattling along the tracks, the streets lined by rows of unkempt brick tenements, the cold-water flats with the communal bathroom, the constant battle with lice, bedbugs, and dirt. No less memorable were the sweet smell of challah baking in the oven, relatives gathered around the Seder table, trips to the library for books and to the rooming house in the Catskills for a short vacation. A subway ticket downtown brought a shy, curious twelve-year-old within reach of the Museum of Natural History, the Metropolitan Museum, and the Metropolitan Opera. Fifty cents guaranteed standing room behind the orchestra section and a taste of operatic magic. Hunter College offered in effect a free college education. Just beyond, New York's Ivy League school, Columbia University, beckoned, willing by the 1930s to admit a few Jews as students even if it would not yet hire them as faculty.

But what to do with this budding intellect? This was the child of an impoverished man who had arrived at Ellis Island with a suitcase containing religious books and an over-burdened mother who taught her daughter to read at the age of four when she herself knew little English. Yet the mother who bragged to the neighbors about the A's on Ruthie's report cards and sent her son—much the poorer student of the two—to dental school after he graduated from college, was also the mother who "redecorated" the apartment to make it presentable for beaus when her daughter turned sixteen. If the signals were mixed, so be it. The imperatives of both Jewish and American culture pointed daughters in one direction—marriage and family.

Daughters with other aspirations found little support. Feminism as an organized movement had virtually disappeared by the 1930s and with it the pressure for equal rights that had inspired an earlier generation of activists. In the years between 1920 and 1960, the proportion of women attending colleges and universities actually declined, as did the proportion of women on college faculties. In addition, the Great Depression and World War II placed extraordinary stresses on the American family. A depressed economy meant delayed marriage, deferred children, unemployed male heads of household. War brought further disruption. With victory came the threat of global annihilation. Yearning for a return to "normalcy," Americans were eager to establish families, discover suburbia, and embrace the familiar roles of housewife and breadwinner, hoping to find in the private sphere of home and family the security that eluded them in the larger world.

Popular magazines and movies reinforced this resurgent

domesticity. While there were stories of "exceptional" women
whose lives were not defined by family alone, women's magazines extolled the joys of the housewife-mother who lovingly
tended to her garden and her bumper crop of children. Even
the heroines hawked by Hollywood in the 1950s fell into two
categories: sex objects and wives. Gone were the brainy, resourceful, independent working women of an earlier era. Depicted in their stead were lonely, frustrated neurotics whose
unhappiness signified the futility of sacrificing domesticity for
a career—a measure of how thoroughly Freudianism had per-
meated Cold War culture.

Experts on female nature, influenced by an influx of European psychoanalysts fleeing Hitler, revived the Freudian
belief that a woman's anatomy was indeed her destiny. According to the Freudian psychiatrist Helene Deutsch, "whenever the young girl exchanges a rich emotional life for scientific thinking, it is to be expected that later in her life sterility
will take the place of motherliness even if she has given birth
to many children." "Normal femininity" meant that a woman
accepted her distinctive sexuality, repressed her "masculine"
strivings, and related to the outside world through identification with husband and children, eschewing intellectual activities. Ferdinand Lundberg and Marynia Farnham made the
case even more boldly in their 1947 best-seller, *Modern
Woman: The Lost Sex*. Tracing feminism to the neurotic im-
pulses of women seeking a share of masculine power because
they had been victims of child abuse, Lundberg and Farnham
cautioned women not to imitate men. Rather, the modern
woman must accept her femininity and find fulfillment
through subordination to her husband and acceptance of
motherhood. Higher education and careers, they warned,
would lead to the "masculinization of women with enormously
dangerous consequences...." The choice was stark: well-ad-
justed homemaker or feminist neurotic. In an era in which
long-term individual therapy acquired unprecedented popu-
larity, helping the unhappy woman to give up her "masculine"

strivings and accept what was said to be her basic feminine nature could take years, as Glater would unfortunately discover.

Cultural imperatives have clearly changed since a tiny cohort of female scientists sought entry to the profession in the 1950s, in part because of the resurgence of an organized feminist movement. Yet that generation's struggle to create a feminine identity combining both love and work, family and career, is one which will resonate with every woman who has faced the same challenge. In this respect, Ruth Bobrov Glater's story, though shaped by the particulars of her own time and circumstances, is in fact the story of Every Woman—every woman of ability and ambition who has yearned for a laboratory, a lecture podium, a judge's chambers, or an operating room of her own. We all have much to learn from her experience.

JANE SHERRON DE HART
University of California, Santa Barbara

INTRODUCTION

It is an unnerving experience to sit down with a fresh pad of paper and a newly sharpened pencil to begin to express the meaning of my life, a life which is rapidly approaching its end. I know this by the sheer force of numbers. I am coming on to my late seventies, truly a heap of years. Statistically, considering my medical history, I have far exceeded my chances of survival. My long life has been intricately woven into the patterns of many other lives, those of my departed parents, my brother, my husbands, my children, my lovers, my friends, my co-workers, my enemies. I have loved and I have hated, both intensely. A fire still burns in me. My voice still rises passionately when I speak of the inequities in the world, of the injustice, the violence, the misery of the poor and homeless, the amorality and mediocrity of so-called world leaders, the laws that favor the few, and on and on. But despite all this, I have reached a peaceful plateau in my emotional life. I know myself to be a good person, incapable of wittingly inflicting pain on others, recognizing evil in the world, yet maintaining my equilibrium in spite of it. However, in this eighth decade of my life I am developing, more each day, an intolerance for idle chatter. Often, when with friends, I disappear into a witnessing mode. My mind goes on automatic. "Enough of this," I say to myself. "Enough idle talk that leads nowhere." I tune out because time is of the essence and the message I wish to leave behind is urgent. My desperate desire is "now to sit or never by the side of the pale-faced moon." My life's denouement is to place the pieces of my life into an organized collage, the beautiful side by side with the ugly, the order with the disorder, the symphony with the cacophony. If I write what is in my heart and head, perhaps the pieces will fall into sensible order and I may leave behind something more than a headstone. Perhaps a guide for those who journey on a while longer than I.

My father is the inspiration for this book. As far back as I remember I would often hear him say in his broken English: "Ven I retire, I vill write a book about myself." But he died and no book was written, not even a single page. All I have of him is what I remember and treasure, the few stories he told me of his childhood and the warmth and love he unstintingly gave me all his life. At eighty, he suffered a cerebral hemorrhage and never regained consciousness. I went to the hospital. I remember the sun streaming in through a large window behind his bed, filling the room with heavenly light. It was a small room, bare except for the narrow bed on which he lay, the sheets neatly tucked in, unruffled, snowy-white, the color of his sweet face. Only his bald head was exposed. I leaned down to kiss him. He lay there unmoving, barely breathing, eyes closed. I could do nothing to help this man whom I had adored all my life, this gentle, giving man who had not fulfilled his dream to write.

I never wanted to lose Papa. But through my tears and grief I understood the inevitability of death. Now, as I approach the twilight of my own life, I am aware of how small and inconsequential we are in the enormity of this universe. And I understand that love between people is really all that matters. It is a heavy toll we pay for this love. And though his departure has left me with an emptiness in my heart, I would not trade anything in the world for the love my father taught me and the sweet, tender memories I hold of him. They are his magnificent gift. I write this book in memory of the Reverend Jacob Bobrov, my beloved father.

Most of my life has been a difficult uphill climb, largely because in my formative years, the early to mid-1900s, society steadfastly refused to recognize the changing needs of women. Traditionally women had been directed toward the subservient, domestic role. The woman who wished to take a different path, perhaps to use her mind and talent to add to world knowledge rather than solely to world population, was belittled and excluded. If she insisted on "being different," she was seen as abandoning her feminine duties and encroaching on forbidden masculine ground. Further, she was ridiculed for her "penis envy" in an era which used Freud's explanation of female "inferiority" with little appreciation of the denigratory nature of his terminology. The "normal" role dictated a woman to marry, bear children, and keep the home fires burning for husband and family.

Although I have always been a feminist, the women's movement of the late 1960s and 1970s came too late to make a difference in my professional life. It has, however, created opportunities for younger women in the sciences, although their continued underrepresentation underscores the relevance of my own unfulfilled aspirations. Usually people who write their autobiographies are those who have achieved some measure of fame, who have achieved their goals in life. But failure too can instruct.

From the heart I wish to thank those people who believed in me and my cause, who affirmed me and spurred me on in my writing.

Thanks to Benjamin J. Cohen, who, though an accomplished academician and author, took time from his work to treat me with gentle respect and constructive criticism as I struggled to put my thoughts on paper.

Thanks to Jane De Hart, who convinced me I had something to say about women's struggle in the sciences. An established scholar whose field of expertise is U.S. women's history, she pointed me to social, psychological, and historical literature that helped me understand my own difficulties and disappointments in the context of others who had undergone similar experiences. She also taught me the value of an answering machine for a writer who wishes to work without interruption.

To my love, Armando Quiros, ever the exquisite therapist and healer, who by his compassion, insight, and nurturance changed the course of my life and made me proud to be the person I am today.

Thanks to Mary James, who patiently, painstakingly processed my voluminous pages of illegible handwriting into a clean computer printout…and with nary a whimper.

Thanks to the librarians at the reference desk of the Santa Barbara Public Library who, time and again, through the three long years of my writing, procured all manner of obscure bits of information at my request—facts I desperately needed to validate and corroborate the words I was writing.

Some years ago Horace Mann said, "We must be ashamed to die until we have won some victory for mankind." This book is my final dissertation and my final hope. Perhaps it will win some small victory for womankind, for *mankind*, indeed for all humanity.

SLAM

THE

DOOR

GENTLY

Childhood

I was born on the eleventh of August, 1919, into the seething ghetto that was the Bronx, New York City, just as the twentieth century came roaring around the bend. As an infant I was certainly not conscious that I was born in a place where the rights of women did not equal those afforded men. The Nineteenth Amendment to the Constitution, the Women's Suffrage Act, did not see the light of day until August 18, 1920, one year and one week after my birth.

I remember 500 Brook Avenue well. I was born on the third floor of a small, dark walk-up tenement. My mother told me that I left her womb very early on a Monday morning, just a few minutes past midnight. I was born in the kitchen. Believable or not, I have the vague memory of a large kitchen with a black iron stove and a small window. This was the room into which I entered the world.

Papa owned a butcher shop on the ground level of the apartment house in which we lived. Although not a butcher, he needed work which permitted him to observe the Jewish Sabbath, which starts at sundown on Friday and ends at sundown on Saturday. Owning a kosher butcher shop permitted him to do so. He would close the store mid-afternoon on Friday, *Erev Shabbat*, then attend services at the synagogue on Friday night and Saturday morning. The Sabbath was holy, a day of cleansing, of purifying one's soul. On this day, as an Orthodox Jew, he did no work. No member of the family was permitted to clean or cook or purchase or exchange money. Even walking was limited. Mostly it was a day to rest, to thank God for the week just past, to refresh one's spirit, to meet friends in the park or visit with family. It was a peaceful, un-eventful day during which one garnered energy to face the coming week.

In our home, at sundown of the Shabbat, a small cold meal called *seudah shlishit* (obligatory third meal) was served. Usually it consisted of cold borscht or *schav*, maybe some cold potatoes with a dab of sour cream, and a cup of tea. Hot *tchai* was always a fitting end to a peaceful Shabbat. On Friday in the late afternoon, Mother would have left one burner of the stove on a very low setting so we could warm a morsel of cold food or prepare tea during the day, should we wish.

As night began to fall and three stars appeared in the sky, Papa would bid farewell to the Shabbat by reciting the Havdalah prayer. Then, in song, we would wish one another *"Shavua tov, a gute Woch, a gesunte Woch"*—a good week, a healthy week. Then Papa was free to go to work, to cut and sell meat and chickens for the few remaining dark hours of the day. Mama went with him.

On the window of the store, in large, gold-colored He-brew letters, was written *"Basar Kasher."* Read from right to left, as Hebrew is, it translated to "Kosher Meat." Below it, in smaller English letters read from left to right, it said Rev. Jacob Bobrov. Jewish law dictated that Orthodox Jews eat only kosher meat, that is, the meat of animals slaughtered by a ritually trained *schochet* under rabbinic supervision. A *schochet*, one hierarchical step beneath a rabbi, was entitled Reverend. Papa was such a one.

Papa's business was brisk. Most Jews in those days, re-cently arrived from Eastern Europe, diligently observed the laws of *kashrut*. They kept kosher. On one particular Sabbath, the day before my birth, Mama was dragging. Though full with child, she did not rest but went downstairs to help Papa in the store. I suspect she did not trust Papa to carry on busi-ness profitably without her. He really was not an entrepre-neur. A man of the book, Papa was honest to a fault. Mama was not so. She knew many tricks to turn a penny—leaving a little extra fat on the meat, not removing the entire bone, selling day-old stock. She was not dishonest, only shrewd. I disliked this in her. I was more like Papa.

My first clear memory is of lying in a baby carriage in the butcher shop. There was a hood on the top of the buggy. I remember darkness there. Women came into the shop and stopped to peek at me. I remember their large faces. I remember also the sweet, pleasurable taste of the rubber nipple on the bottle of milk Mama had hastily shoved into my mouth. Mama did not breast feed me. Either she had no milk or no time, I don't know which.

It is Friday, late afternoon, and Papa is preparing for the Sabbath. He is cleaning the store. The floor has been swept and fresh sawdust has been spread on the worn wooden boards. I like the clean, sweet smell of the wood shavings. The sun is beginning to descend from its height in the sky. It is warm and comforting. I am sitting on the big, snowy-white marble slab inside the wide store window eating half an apple with a teaspoon; I have no teeth strong enough to pierce the apple's skin. Above me are meat hooks all in a row. During the busy week these hold ritually slaughtered, plucked chickens for sale, dripping blood. Now the hooks are empty and clean. With a steel brush, Papa is scraping the butcher block, the klutz. I am four years old and in childish bliss. I have no responsibilities. A warm euphoric feeing pervades my mind and body. I am surrounded by cleanliness. The busy work week which keeps Mama and Papa from me is winding down. Blessed Sabbath is approaching with its peace and quiet, and I can be with Mama and Papa and my big brother, Solly, without interruption.

Now, a few days past Shabbat, Solly has been bitten by a dog. There is a flurry of excitement as Mama rushes off to take him to the hospital.

"Stay home," she says to me, as I move toward the door

with them.

"I'm afraid alone, Mama," I say, tears filling my eyes.

"Papa is downstairs in the store, *daige nisht*, don't worry," she says, dashing out the door with Solly in tow.

I sit at the window ledge with my make-believe train, an upside-down hair brush. "Woo-woo," I say in a tremulous voice, hitting the brush's handle as it rapidly moves forward. "Woo-woo," I say, trying distraction to comfort myself. When will they come back? Will Solly die? Time drags. Finally, voices! They are home!

"Mama! Solly!" I cry out, racing to greet them.

Solly has a bandaged knee, but he is not crying. He is very brave. I did not know then that he would carry a scar on his leg all the remaining days of his short life.

I had a black fox terrier we called Dog. My parents, concerned with more important matters, did not bother to give him a name. Naming a dog was frivolous compared to serious work, they said. Still, I loved that little beast who slept at the foot of my bed each night. Suddenly one day he disappeared.

"A car hit Dog," Mama explained without emotion. "He's dead."

"But, Mama," I cried, "I loved Dog so much."

She gave me a hard, cold stare. There was no further discussion.

We also had a cat. She lived in the butcher shop, not in our house. She also had no name. We called her Pussy. She was not really a pet like Dog. Her purpose in life was to catch mice in the butcher shop. She lived well, ate heartily. In addition to mice, there were a lot of chicken entrails available to her. Behind the store was a well-hidden alley into which nobody ventured except Pussy and some tomcats. There she had her trysts. There she bore her kittens regularly, like clockwork, "one damned kitten after another." Soon after they were born, Papa put the kittens in a sack and turned them loose in nearby St. Ann's Park. That is what he told me.

Occasionally I heard cats wailing and moaning in the back alley. Why were they fighting with one another? It took some years before I learned that sexual things were happening back there, but nobody gave me an explanation.

When I was four I had a little playmate, Tessie Tannenbaum. She lived in an apartment house a few doors down from 500 Brook Avenue. Her house had a long, long flight of steps which led up to the large front door. On each side of the steps ran a coarse, black iron handrail. Many times a day we amused ourselves by flying up and down those stairs, hanging on to the rails. And then one day Tessie left me and went off to kindergarten.

The school, an architecturally grim, squalid red-brick building, was around the corner from where we lived. I followed Tessie there. It was no fun to stay home alone without her. Besides, I could already read a bit.

Children took toys from a closet, sat down at low tables, and started to play. I helped myself to a box of colored pegs and a pegboard, sat myself down in a pint-sized chair at a pint-sized table, and began to make designs with the pegs. It was fun. I loved being there. I loved the smell of the school, the order.

Suddenly, the teacher entered the room. She looked around, then riveted her attention on me.

"Who are you?" she asked, towering over me.

"I'm Ruthie Bobrov," I answered, my voice quivering.

"What are you doing here?"

"I came to school with my friend Tessie Tannenbaum."

"I'm sorry, you'll have to leave. You are not registered in school. You are too young. Go home."

I was heartbroken. School drew me like a magnet. Out I went to home, around the corner to nothing. Nobody to talk to, nobody to play with. "Someday I'll tell Mama to take me to school and talk to that mean teacher," I promised myself. "Right now she's too busy in the butcher shop."

•

Five hundred Brook Avenue was close to St. Ann's Park and close also to the only two truly substantial buildings in the neighborhood, St. Mary's Church and Rupert's Brewery. Each hour one could hear the doleful church bells sounding the time of day. From the windows of our meager cold-water flat I could see the brewery across the street. It was shut down because of Prohibition.

It was a forbidding sight, a dirty, block-long brick building with huge floor-to-ceiling windows boarded over with coarse, heavy wooden slats. On the periphery of the building men were lying in the street. Were they dead? Were they dying? My child's mind, terrified by this sight, could not comprehend. I did not understand drunkenness, although my father often spoke against it with anger and ridicule.

As I grew older, I often wondered about these sad souls. Why did grown men behave that way? It seemed they would have alcohol as a baby would have milk. And if not ethyl alcohol, then wood alcohol, methyl alcohol, turpentine, witch hazel, or any other intoxicating liquid would do. Day after day they returned to the decaying old brewery, bottle in hand.

My contempt (or was it fear?) of alcohol and alcoholics manifested itself when I was about six. Mother took me downtown to S. Klein on the Square to buy me a winter coat. Downtown meant a long subway ride from the east Bronx where we lived to 14th Street in Manhattan. This was a rare treat; it meant an outing with Mama.

S. Klein on the Square, a store about a block square and perhaps three or four stories high, contained a hodgepodge of women's clothing. Chaos on the Square might have been a more appropriate name for the place. Here women came from all over New York City and elsewhere to buy cheap. The huge building was filled with rack upon rack, floor upon floor, of coats, dresses, and suits in all sizes and styles, all intermingled and only vaguely marked as to size or price. One had to hunt diligently for one's bargains. Luckily, Mother found me a *number*. It was a brown coat with large cape sleeves and a black belt. I looked like Bat-child in it. It was truly ugly, but it was cheap. Mother had little time or patience to spend sifting through the millions (or so it seemed) of garments to find me a truly attractive coat. Utilitarian, durable, and inexpensive was good enough.

As Mama and I sat together in the subway train bumping along on the way home, a staggering drunk sauntered by and stopped in front of us. Reaching up, he grabbed an overhead strap, straining to keep himself upright. Mama had started graying early, and by now her hair was almost pure white. The drunk focused his attention on her. Perhaps, in the dim recesses of his foggy mind, he remembered his own mother. Standing there in front of us, weaving crazily as the train shook from side to side, he began singing "Mother Machree," off-key, his eyes rolling around in his head. To me he was a despicable sight. The train rumbled into a station, came to a stop, and the door swung open. I dashed out the door to escape him. As the door began to close, Mother was barely able to catch me to drag me back. I have been a teetotaler all my life.

Brook Avenue was within spitting distance of the Third Avenue "L." There, in the shadow of the elevated trains, lived very few English-speaking adults. Only the little street urchins like myself spoke English—gutter English, that is. We were, after all, first-generation Americans who had no proper English-speaking models at home. Our parents came from Europe—Italy, Russia, Ireland, Poland. The only adults I knew who spoke proper English were the postman and the policeman and, later, my kindergarten teacher. Their families must have come over on the *Mayflower*. In most instances, our first language was the mother tongue of our parents. My first language was Yiddish. My parents refused to speak Russian because they hated the land from which they had come.

I remember those early years of my life spent in the filth and squalor of the ghetto which the poor, newly arrived immigrants regarded as heaven. From what hell had they been released that a dingy walk-up flat with no hot water and a communal bathroom at the end of a long, dark hall was home sweet home?

I cannot speak of other places in New York because I knew only the Bronx. Here we were a heterogeneous gaggle of young ruffians. We knew nothing yet of gentility, beauty, or culture. Most of the American adults in our neighborhood were, as my father haughtily called them, *am ha-aretz*, people of the earth—dirty, rough, uncultured, uneducated clods. Papa had brought with him across the ocean the notion, intact from the Russian Jewish *shtetl*, that an educated man has *yikhes* (status), while a manual laborer is a social disgrace.

My formal education started with kindergarten at age five. Our teachers were all gentrified second- and third-generation Yankee Americans, mostly of Irish descent, who spoke fluent English. We kids could barely understand them, nor they us. Our ilk was not represented in the school administration.

Prejudice was rampant in the New York City public schools. Wop, polak, kike, spik, nigger were slurs we often heard. However, as a small child, I didn't feel the pain and stigma much because *de facto* segregation was in full bloom and we Jews were really a majority in our own small, restricted ghetto. Our classes were homogeneous, all Jews, except for the teachers. This did not seem to trouble our immigrant parents at all; they felt comfortable that their children did not need to mingle with Christians. Nor were they interested in stirring up trouble with the school administration. To me, my polished WASP teachers were the minority. They lived elsewhere—who knows where? They lived differently. It wasn't until I reached puberty and ventured out into the world that stretched beyond the Bronx that I began to notice how strange I was, how different my clothes, my behavior, my speech. And then shame, embarrassment, and humiliation set in. My education was already rapidly distancing me from the European culture of my Jewish parents. I had not yet learned the new American way. It was a dilemma.

When I was four, we moved to a second dirty old tenement a few blocks away from the butcher shop and the house of my birth. Mama worked in the butcher shop with Papa. She left for work early in the morning. Some of the time I spent with my brother, Solly, but a good deal of time I spent alone. Solly, five years older than I, wanted little to do with his kid sister. He went his way, the leader of a gang of boys, all approximately his age. He was a Pied Piper; his friends followed wherever he went and did whatever he dictated. They were not delinquents, merely high-energy kids totally absorbed in play. Girls were an annoyance to them, and I, a girl, was a burr under Solly's saddle. "You're just a little fat horse," he would tell me. "Keep out of my way." His treatment did nothing to help my sense of self as a female.

One day, something happened which assured me that not only was one a pest if one was a girl, but that being a girl was dangerous.

On the ground floor, under the stairwell in our apartment building, was an empty space. One morning, as I came flying down the stairs to play, a few little boys were lying there in wait for me. They were not part of Solly's rat pack, somewhat younger. As I reached ground, they attacked. They pinned me to the ground, pulled down my pants and, one after another, as I fought to catch my breath and screamed to get free, felt around in my vagina. I was outraged.

The next day I waited on the stoop for these budding hoodlums to appear. As one came out the door, I jumped him, flattening him to the ground. Then I started pummeling him with all the strength in my little four-year-old body. Solly and his friends gathered round, shouting and cheering me on.

"Beat him up, Ruthie," they called. "Knock the shit out of him, Ruthie. Kill him."

Neither Solly nor anybody else offered to help me fight my battle. Nobody interfered. Soon I could no longer hold the squealing, wriggling worm of a kid down. He got free and ran.

Then I went to the butcher shop to tell my mother my sad tale.

I was full of shame and humiliation, but I did not cry. I was not punished, nor did I deserve to be. But neither was I consoled or comforted. Early in life I learned that my struggles were my own to handle. Very, very early I learned that I was easy prey for attack by males and that I, because I was female, must be ever vigilant.

The Bronx was truly not a place for a fun childhood. Row upon row of old, poorly constructed, dirty, gray- or red-brick tenements lined the streets, story upon story of apartments piled one on top of another, three, five, some six levels high, with rarely even a narrow alley or passageway between. Families lived in small, confined apartments, each room a tiny space barely the size of a legitimate closet. We lived like rats in overcrowded cages.

The sidewalks were gray cement lined with stinking garbage cans, the streets narrow and noisy all day. Here young women strolled with baby carriages. Here old women, some wearing wigs or *scheitlach*, in accordance with European Jewish tradition, could be seen sitting on portable folding chairs, or standing about gossiping, or ambling through the streets.

There in St. Ann's Park close by one could see green grass, trees, and a few flowers come spring, but, aside from these, very little else grew except for an occasional brave, little Wandering Jew which miraculously came up between the cracks in the cement sidewalks. When, on occasion, the little blue flowers showed their faces, my child heart would sing. They were the only signs of beauty in the otherwise drab street. How did they manage to survive and bloom without care, without love, without water? Because of its name, Wandering Jew (*Commelina communis*), and where it grew, I felt close kinship with it. I, too, felt like an unnoticed, uncared-for flower growing between the cracks in the hard cement of a hostile city. We were both survivors. And people paid no attention to either of us.

However, there was one tree which all New Yorkers knew but to which they paid little attention. It had the unlikely name, Tree of Heaven (*Ailanthus altissima*). It grew unplanted, untended in the vacant lots behind the tenements, broken glass and garbage strewn around its base. There, in the shade of the spreading canopy of the Tree of Heaven, in the barren, hard soil through which the tree managed to grow, to sucker and seed, we kids played innocently and unsupervised. There we found our small treasures among the shards, the rusting cans, and other bits of abandoned debris.

My beautiful mother was totally unaware of her good looks. Nor, had she known, would it have made any difference to her. She was primarily the staunch matriarch, the head of all her family. Her siblings, three sisters and two brothers, all sought her advice and guidance. No major decision was made until my mother was consulted. And she ruled with a strong hand dominated by her very disciplined, keen mind. She controlled, not frigidly but austerely and with measured reason. Speak with any member of her family but me, and you will hear praises for Mama's intelligence, her caring, her compassion, her warmth. But I knew her from the womb. She was not warm and tender to me. This made me a very sad little girl yearning for love from Mama. In an attempt to obtain some warmth, I would snuggle up to her whenever she permitted it, which was not often. I would lay my head on her lap and plead, "Please, Mama, stroke my *kepe*." Hesitantly, almost with distaste, she would run her fingers through my curly black hair for a few brief minutes. Then, suddenly, as if a magnet were pulling from behind, she would give me a swift shove away. God, how this hurt my child soul! Her stroking was never much, never often, never soft, never pleasurably given.

One Sunday afternoon the entire family gathered at our house, my aunts, uncles, cousins, all our maternal family who lived close by. Mama prepared a yummy meal of Jewish delicatessen—hot sliced corned beef, rye bread, kosher salami, hot dogs on rolls with sauerkraut and mustard, garlic pickles, and Heinz's kosher baked beans in a big pot.

What a feast! What smells! What fun! I looked forward to savoring this food, which we were permitted only on special occasions. Mama seemed happy, freely dishing out food to all her guests. But she didn't invite me to the table. Patiently I waited for her to ask me what I would like to eat. She served all the adults first, then my kid cousins, Izzy, Carl, and Ruthie, then my brother, Solly. What about me? I was the youngest and smallest child there. Satisfied that everybody had been served, she began to fill her own plate. Still I was not asked. She was unaware she had overlooked me. Tears streaming down my face, my little heart breaking at being unnoticed and therefore unnecessary, I tugged at the back of her dress.

"Mama," I said, "you didn't serve me!"

"Oh," she said unconcernedly, "*was willst du zum essen?*"

"*Gur nisht*, nothing," I answered and ran into another room to be with myself and my anguish.

My heart was broken. But in her cold, proud austerity she did not follow me nor urge me to come back. I have never forgotten the sense of worthlessness I experienced that day. That was my mother, generous to all but me.

Both my parents had left Russia in 1904. They did not know one another at that time, and arrived in America by different routes. Mama came with her father, their ship docking in Galveston, Texas. Papa came alone. His ship docked at Ellis Island. They met, an arranged *shiddach* (marriage match) several years later in New York. Both of them shared a hatred for Russia, for all things Russian, and for all things gentile. This was a natural consequence of their having been born and raised under the Romanov czarist yoke with its open, widely accepted hatred of Jews. Jews were outcasts. They could never hope to achieve stability or equality there. They lived in constant, unrelenting fear of attack.

At the age of two, Papa had lost both parents to some unnamed disease. There was no money for doctors or medicine in the *shetl* in Russia. Certainly no doctors were available to poor Jews without money. In any event, Jews were expendable. My father's family was poor, living from hand to mouth in a small village, Berezin, in White Russia. Papa's father had been a *schochet*, a Reverend. His parents' demise left him totally alone at a very tender age. He survived by spending days in the *yeshiva* and nights by *teg*.

The *yeshiva* was a place in every Eastern European community where men met to sit and study and discuss Torah and Talmud. Here, in these houses of study and worship, all matters were discussed: God, faith, *mazel*, *Yiddishkeit*, good and evil, and the latest *umglicken* (atrocities) that were occurring under the czar. Any discussions critical of the czar were punishable by imprisonment. In Papa's day, in the middle to late 1800s, the law permitted no secular matters to be discussed in the *yeshiva*, only matters specifically Jewish.

Come nightfall, young Papa would leave the *yeshiva* to eat a meager meal and spend the night in some charitable person's modest home, a practice called *teg* (days). The poor forlorn tot would wander the yeshiva by day; by night he was allowed a crust of bread and a straw mattress on which to sleep by somebody's fire. Winters in Russia were cruel, and food was scarce. As a result of his pitiful life of starvation and want, Papa developed rickets and grew to be a very small adult, almost stunted, with a caved-in chest.

However, serendipitously, his caved-in chest saved him from what he considered a fate worse than death. When he was eighteen, he was ordered to report to the army for military service. For anybody, the czar's army was miserable, cruel, and corrupt, but for Jews it was hell. Anti-Semitism was openly condoned and sadistically, gleefully practiced. But my small, clever father managed to avoid conscription. He found a way to bribe the chief doctor with a ten-ruble note.

A committee of several doctors, which was to examine him and rule on his eligibility for the military, sat at a long table, the chief doctor at the head. When Papa entered the room, the bribee looked derisively at the little stunted, frightened Jew and said, "*N'yet*...no good...he has tuberculosis. Look at that pitiful chest. Hear him cough." Papa obligingly coughed.

The doctors began a dispute amongst themselves. "He's good enough. Who cares about his cough? Let him cough. We'll take him."

"*N'yet*," insisted the chief, and, while they were arguing noisily amongst themselves, Papa surreptitiously slipped out a side door into the woods and hid.

That night, under cover of darkness, Papa stole across the *grenitz*, the border, into Poland. From there he made his way, only God knows how and by what route, into a port city in England and from there on a ship to America. His courageous story will never be known in its entirety; he never told me how or where he obtained a passport. But even as a very small child I cheered in my heart, as I still do today, for my brave little father and his caved-in chest.

Like most Russian Jews, my mother also came to America from poverty. As were many Hebraically educated Jews in Eastern Europe, her father was also a *schochet*. But he found it necessary to augment his income by making and repairing shoes in the small *shtetl* of Berisiv, White Russia, close to Berezin where Papa was born. Mama's misery was somewhat less than Papa's. At least she had living parents.

I am eternally grateful to both my mother and father for having had the courage and wisdom to leave Russia in 1904. Had it not been for their bravery in crossing the vast Atlantic to an unknown world, I might have been born and died in Russia at the hands of the Russians or the Nazis along with all those members of my family who had remained there, and as did millions of my fellow Jews.

My father's sister, Sprintze, remained behind in Russia when Papa left for America. Although the Russian Revolution was already in full swing in 1923, my father was, somehow, able to rescue his sister's twenty-year-old son, Abe Cohen, and bring him to America.

Abe came to live with us in New York until he could establish himself. Four years old, I immediately fell in love with him. He was full of fun, playful and warm, and he wore pince-nez, which fascinated me. Whenever he came home from work, he would bring, especially for me, a package of Wrigley's Juicy Fruit gum.

One day I did something or other which displeased my mother. She grabbed me, flung me bottom-side-up across her lap and began to spank me hard and uncontrollably. She was sitting in a rocking chair, and each blow set the chair in vigorous motion.

"*Vayne*," she screamed at me in Yiddish. "Cry! I will not stop until you cry!"

But I refused to cry; in my mind I had done nothing seriously wrong. She continued to strike. Finally, unable to withstand the punishment, one of the legs of the rocking chair gave way with a groan. Mother faltered for a moment, but only for a moment, and then she returned to her spanking.

Just then Abe returned home from work. "Tante Jennie!" he cried. "Stop! *Vos tust du?*"

His words broke into her consciousness and, her hand still held high ready to strike again, she relaxed her grip on me.

I saw my opportunity. Jumping from her lap, I grabbed the gum Abe held out to me, dashed out of the dining room, through the bedroom, through the window, and out onto the fire-escape. There I sat to lick my wounds and enjoy the sweet taste of Abe's gift. As I rushed out Abe had given my *kepe* a loving stroke. That was the last time Mama ever hit me.

Papa, on the other hand, unquestionably loved me. I knew this because he never raised his voice to me, never spoke to me in anger, never struck me. "Rutele," he would often say, "*du bist a gute maidele*, a good child." He tried always to honor whatever small request I might make of him. Yet he would not hug me or hold me close. I suppose it was his Talmudic training that had taught him never to hold a female

close to his body except his wife. Occasionally he kissed me
and gave me a small pat. But he was disdainful and critical of
my uncle Joe, who always held his daughter, my cousin
Beatrice, on his lap and caressed her, even when she had
reached eighteen years of age and older. It repelled Papa, and
he spoke openly against this. I was also repelled by it, first
perhaps out of jealousy and later, as I grew older, because it
smacked of incest. But in my innermost heart, as a little girl, I
wished one or both of my parents would hold me close, even
if only a little bit.

When I grew up and was better able to comprehend, I
understood that Mama was incapable of acting more warmly
toward me. She was a product of her own loveless childhood.
When she was but a child in Russia, she was, as the oldest, the
appointed caretaker of her six siblings. One of her brothers
had died of diphtheria while yet a baby. Did my mother take
responsibility for this tragedy? I wonder. Perhaps this event
added further to her withdrawal from warmth. Her mother
could not—or would not—handle the household nor the children. When I came to know my grandmother, after she had
already been in America for several years, she was more than
cold; she was a solid block of ice. Her childhood must have
been as bleak as the Russian winters she lived through,
though my grandmother never spoke of it. She and I never
had a discussion about anything or anyone.

I remember my maternal grandmother as an invalid who
never left the bed unless lifted bodily into a wheelchair by a
strong adult. I remember her as either supine in bed or
slouched in her wheelchair. Early in her life, after the birth of
seven children in rapid succession, she had retired to bed with
severe arthritis. Perhaps she had had enough of her harsh life.
But the more time she spent in bed, the stiffer and more im-
mobile her joints became and the less she could move.

Bube (my grandmother) and Zaida (my grandfather) lived
with my Aunt Ella and her husband, Uncle Ben, in one large
apartment. My grandparents' bedroom was a bleak, un-

decorated room, so small that it was almost completely filled by two twin beds and a dresser.

Once a week, without fail, I visited my grandparents with my parents, not out of love, rather out of duty. No love seemed to pass between my grandmother and grandfather, nor did any obvious love flow from them to their children— my mother, Jennie; my aunts, Minnie, Ella, and Sarah; and my uncles, Henry and Sam. And certainly they never showed love to any of their eleven grandchildren. I was in my early teens when they died, and I did not mourn their passing.

So Mother came by her coldness naturally. When my aunts and uncles spoke of Jennie's warmth, it was because she was the only mother they could remember. I am sorry I could not have given Mama the love she so desperately needed, but by the time I came along, it was probably too late. Neither she nor I ever understood one another's emotional needs.

While my mother could not give me the gift of love, she did give me the wonderful gift of reading. When I was four she began to teach me to read, painstakingly, slowly, and patiently. This was a minor miracle because she was illiterate in English. But having herself been deprived of an education, she understood and appreciated the importance of literacy, and together we learned to read.

From the time of my birth, my mother worked in the butcher shop, shoulder to shoulder with Papa. But when I reached five, Papa sold the store and Mama was at home, and there was the good smell of food cooking and, on Friday afternoons, the delightful aroma of baking bread. In preparation for the Shabbat each week, Mama would bake *challah*, a traditional delicious, sweet, white, soft bread. And she would spend time with me.

Often during the week she and I would take long walks together to the library for books. Long live Andrew Carnegie, who with 350 million dollars endowed 2,500 libraries as well as other cultural institutions throughout the nation. As a child and well into my education, I was the eager, grateful beneficiary of his good will.

One day, on our way home from the library, a sudden storm broke. All around us thunder roared and lightening flashed. In the downpour we ran, protecting the books under our arms as best we could.

By the time we reached home, we were soaked to the skin. I threw off my wet clothes and, in my underwear, climbed on top of the unmade bed with its huge old Russian pillows full of chicken feathers. My books in my lap, I started to leaf through the pages. What joy for me! Fairy tales with pictures! How I enjoyed browsing and reading with the rain pouring down outside, making a comforting rhythmic beat against the windows. Away from the world, I was safe with the books. That was when my lifelong love affair with books first began.

It was in 1925 that my mother bought me Clement Moore's magical, wonderful book, *A Visit from St Nicholas*, which started with the famous familiar words, "'Twas the night before Christmas...." Except for my father's few religious Hebrew tomes, which he had managed to bring with him from Russia, books were not purchased in my home; they were borrowed from the public library. So this purchase was a momentous event in my life.

The book was long and narrow, about twelve inches long and seven wide, printed in color on some sort of rigid, celluloid-covered paper. The pages were washable and practically indestructible. We read that book together, Mama and I, and I memorized the poem word for word. How I loved the pictures of the bearded, roly-poly Santa Claus flying over the rooftops and the reindeer-drawn sleigh and the stocking-capped Papa and the stars in the vast sky and the glistening snow. Imagine children asleep expecting wonderful gifts upon awakening...when I had not one toy! Imagine pure white virgin snow covering a lovely landscape...when all I knew was dirty slush as the snow quickly melted and was immediately trampled underfoot as it hit the city streets! Imagine all that beauty, all that warmth and wonder!

Innocently, as children are wont, I associated none of this with things Christian or hostile. "'Twas the night before Christmas and all through the house...." Visions of sugar plums danced in my head. And I knew every reindeer by name—Donder, Blitzen, Dasher, Prancer.... Why had my mother bought me this book about Christmas? Perhaps the pretty colors had caught her eye and appealed to the little child somewhere still alive in her. I am so happy that in her innocence, in spite of her understandable prejudice against gentiles, she bought that book for me.

Papa sold the butcher shop when I was almost five, and we moved to Teller Avenue, a short distance away from where I was born. Papa bought a chicken market which catered to Jewish retail butchers. Again he had found work which permitted him to observe the Sabbath.

The chicken market was a huge one-story building filled with nothing but chicken coops stacked one on top of another, reaching almost to the ceiling. All kinds of chickens were crowded into the coops—white ones, red ones, speckled black-and-white ones. The place stank of chicken shit. In staccato fashion, little chicken heads popped in and out between the slats to peck at corn in small cups hanging at intervals from the coops.

Butchers came. Grabbing a chicken by one leg, they would pull those they wanted from between the slats, the little creatures squawking and struggling against impending slaughter. Papa would hurriedly recite a Hebrew prayer over the chicken. "Blessed art Thou, O Lord our God, King of the universe, who hallows us with Your commandments to slaughter in compliance with Jewish law." With one swift cut, he would slice the chicken's throat. Now the chicken was kosher and fit for Jewish consumption. On to the next victim.

As a very small child I was aware of Papa's devotion to his holy knives. He would take them out of their repository in a bureau drawer in his bedroom. Some knives were short, six inches long. Some were huge, about a foot and a half long. The short ones were used to kill chickens, the large ones for slaughtering cows and sheep. When he first arrived from Europe, Papa had slaughtered cows for Armour and Swift in Kansas City, but now he restricted his practice to chickens. However, he kept all his knives honed, ready for use should the need arise. Each week Papa performed the same ritual. He would sharpen the knives on a pumice stone and then run the fingernail of his right thumb along the sharpened edge. Hebrew law commanded that the knives be razor sharp so as to dispatch the poor creatures quickly with the least amount of suffering. The knives were regularly inspected by rabbis. Not the slightest nick was permitted in a blade. I never did understand why it was only acceptable for Jews to eat chickens and cows that had been slaughtered by a specially ordained man rather than by any ordinary person. Probably the schochet's prayer absolved Jews from the sin of killing one of God's creatures. Mine not to reason why. I hated the chicken market and what occurred there.

But Papa's purchase of the chicken market liberated Mama from the drudgery of the butcher shop, and that made both Mama and me very happy. But our happiness lasted only a few short years until I was seven, when Papa failed at his new enterprise.

Papa had taken on a partner, a Reverend Schorr, but they did not get along. I was too little to understand the details of their disagreement. I only knew the venture was short-lived. During the two to three years of Mama's freedom, until she went back to working in yet another butcher shop with Papa, she spent a lot of time with me, much to my childish delight. I needed her. Those were happy years for me.

But soon there developed a dramatic glitch in this happiness, something over which nobody seemed to have any power. The mid-1920s in New York were the heyday of the booming Lower Eastside mobs—the Black Hand, the

Camorra, the Mafia, and the Unione Siciliano. Meyer Lansky and his young hoodlum friend, Bugsy Siegel, were rapidly climbing their crooked ladder to criminal success. Though they were quite young when Papa bought his market, they were mean enough to strike terror into Papa's heart. Somewhere along their path, they decided to extract protection money from the *schochtim* Union. The fact that the union was a group of religious Jews opposed to violence made no difference to the hoodlums. In fact, it made the *schochtim* easy targets. Most of the *schochtim* were newly arrived immigrants from pogrom-torn Russia. While they understood anti-Semitic Cossacks, they had never before had contact with this new breed of American hoodlum. Papa and his new partner were ordered to pay up or else. Every day Papa brought home another story of violence committed against a person who had crossed Bugsy. Papa could think of no alternative but to pay Bugsy or his henchmen on demand.

Every Sabbath evening, as the day wound down, Papa would leave home on foot to do his *schechita* (slaughtering) at the chicken market, which was within walking distance of our apartment. Normally he would return home by midnight. But with the advent of Bugsy into our lives, we didn't know what to expect. Mama and Solly and I would sit up tremulously waiting for Papa to return. I could hardly keep my eyes from closing until midnight, but neither could I permit myself to sleep. None of us could sleep with the formidable thought that Bugsy or one of his thugs might waylay Papa on his way home. Finally Papa would arrive home breathless, either from fear or hurry, or both. In spite of this, he would always remember to bring home a Baby Ruth candy bar, which he would cut up into small pieces and distribute among us. Papa safely home, we could now permit ourselves to sleep. Bugsy Siegel and the Baby Ruth candy bars stand out clearly in the memory of my young life.

It was September, 1924. I had just turned five the month

before. Mama took me by the hand up the hill from Teller Avenue to school.

My first day in kindergarten, my teacher, Miss Ketchup, said, "Girls, bring one of your dolls to school tomorrow." Which doll was I to bring? I had no doll. I came home full of apprehension.

"Teacher says I must bring a doll to school tomorrow, Mama. What shall I do?"

"We'll go to Bathgate Avenue and buy you a doll," she responded. "Come hurry, before it gets dark."

Bathgate Avenue, a long walk from Teller Avenue, was on the other side of Third Avenue where every few minutes the elevator trains rattled noisily across the tracks. In the shadow of the "L" was Bathgate Avenue, a narrow street lined on each side by dingy shops. Outside the stores were pushcarts and makeshift stands with merchandise piled high, a hodgepodge of fruit, shoes, vegetables, pants, underwear—merchandise of all sorts, all in total disorder. You could find almost anything there if you searched.

We went into a dark, windowless little shop piled high from floor to ceiling with boxes.

"We want to buy a doll," Mama declared matter-of-factly.

The lady clerk reached high and took down two boxes. My heart skipped a beat. This was the first time in my life I had been taken to a store to purchase a toy. I was bug-eyed. How my young life was expanding! My first homework assignment, and it was going to net me a doll! School was going to be a wonderful adventure, I knew.

One doll was large and very beautiful. The other was small and not so elegant. For a little girl who had never before had a doll, I was overwhelmed at the prospect of owning either.

"You may have one or the other," Mother said, turning to me. But to the clerk she said, "How much do they cost?"

She seemed worried about money. I truly wanted the bigger doll. It wore a beautiful pink satin dress, and its eyelids opened and closed. Instead, I chose the small one. So what if her eyes didn't open and close? She was less expensive.

"It will be easier for me to carry the smaller one to school, Mama," I lied, secretly yearning for the larger doll. "The large one will be too heavy."

Delighted with my doll, any doll, I clutched her to my heart all the way home.

When I was about six I received my first and only toy from my father (aside from the doll, which was really a homework assignment). I was in bed with the flu, and Papa bought a surprise to cheer me up. "*Schnell*, open it," he commanded with a twinkle in his eye, handing me a small package from behind his back.

The package rattled as I excitedly tore open the paper wrapping. To my joy…a farm set! There were miniature sheep and cows and chickens and fences and a barn. I could assemble the celluloid pieces and build my farm in any way I wished. I cherished Papa's gift and played with it for hours on end. How I loved my dear, sweet father.

When I returned to school several days later, during art hour the teacher ordered us to make a book cover. She said: "Fold your paper in the middle to look like a book, draw a picture on the front, and give your book a name." Inspired by my farm set, I drew a picture of a farmhouse and barn and trees, and a country road that went up and away over a hill. I entitled my book: "The House by the Side of the Road." In truth, I yearned to leave the ugliness of New York and live in a quiet farmhouse by the side of an unpaved, tree-lined country road.

I do not remember the first grade because I was only there for a few days before I was told to report to the second-grade classroom. I could already read quite well.

The practice in the New York City public school system in and before 1925 was to fire a female teacher should she marry. After all, she no longer needed to work; her husband would support the family. Her responsibility was to stay home, bear and raise children. Consequently my teachers were nearly always spinsters, some few men. My second-grade teacher was Miss Shields, a dour old lady with a long, sad face and gray hair. I was a quiet child, so even without her stern demeanor to control me, I would have been obedient.

Every day my schoolwork earned me a gold star for excellence. By the end of the term, I had won one of the two pencil boxes awarded to the two best students in the class. This was determined on the basis of who had collected the greatest number of stars.

The pencil box was a two-tiered affair made of green, unbendable cardboard. Below, it had a sliding drawer with crayons; above were pencils, a ruler, and an eraser. Never had I possessed anything so magnificent as a cardboard pencil box with a magical sliding drawer. I was overwhelmed.

My family was not given to hyperbole. It seemed quite natural and ordinary to them that I should be an excellent student. They didn't understand my childish insecurity, my need to be commended. They should have celebrated my first academic success with a party, with at least an ice-cream soda at the candy store. But nothing happened. Miss Shields had tried in her impersonal, detached way to let me know my scholastic value by awarding me the pencil box. Since nobody in my family made any fuss over it, it didn't seem all that much of a success. And I kept working harder and harder at school, throwing myself into learning and reading to the exclusion of any form of sociability. I therefore had very little time or wish for friends as I grew up.

Passover was always a time of wonderment and joy for me as a child. The cold winter almost over, I could feel a hint of spring in the air, a promise of green leaves and flowers as buds began to swell.

In the park, the magnolias would soon begin to open their

large, magnificent buds to produce showy white flowers as large as my small head. The white flowers against the dark green twigs was divine art to me. The forsythia bushes would soon burst forth in a mass of yellow flowers, and the lilacs would bloom in patches of lavender, sending forth their incomparably delightful scent. Soon, to my childish joy and anticipation, the leaf buds of all that grew would begin to break, to unfurl their infant pale green leaves to the world. With each spring day, they grew greener until all the dormancy and darkness of winter yielded to the inevitable force of renewed life. The air grew warmer, the sun stronger, and the greenness deepened. How I loved Passover. How I loved the spring!

At the *seder*, Papa from his *hessibet* at the head of the table, would read from the Hagaddah. When he arrived at the Song of Songs, my heart leaped up as I contemplated the oncoming spring with its green newness.

> *For lo, the winter is past.*
> *Flowers appear on the earth*
> *The time of singing is come*
> *The song of the turtledove*
> *Is heard in our land*
> *The fig tree putteth forth her green figs*
> *And the vines in blossom give forth their fragrance.*
> *Arise, my beloved, my fair one*
> *And come away.*

When young, I did not understand the part about "my beloved, my fair one." Papa never stopped long enough to explain it. I learned about this much later. But the promise of spring thrilled me as a child and still does today.

The horde around the *seder* table, my aunts and uncles and cousins, wanted food, not prayer. Papa would push hard to finish his obligatory prayers before the huge traditional meal could be served. "U-kay, U-kay," he would say in his broken English. "I'm goink very fest; like de Tventiet Centery

Limited." But, small as I was, I always resonated to the promise of flowers appearing on the denuded earth and the song of the turtledove. I had never heard the song of a turtledove. But I knew I would soon hear crickets and see polliwogs and frogs in Crotona Park's lake. That was good enough for me. Years later, as my sense of the spiritual grew and matured, I understood the meaning of King Solomon's love. I understood that the poetry of nature and love expressed in the Song of Songs referred to the love-bond between God and His people, Israel. But when I was little, I simply cherished the promise of newness, spring flowers, a new dress, and maybe even, if God were willing, a new spring coat.

From the time I can remember, I had a passion for all things that grew, for green leaves and blossoms. One Sabbath as Papa, Mama, Solly, and I were taking a stroll, we passed a small house in front of which grew a rose bush laden with pink blossoms just out of reach. How I lusted for a rose, only one single rose! Solly the daredevil, always ready to break the rules, offered to jump the spiked iron fence and fetch one for me. But it was the Sabbath, and tearing was forbidden. My first spiritual dilemma—at age six! With tears in my eyes I refused Solly's gallant offer. Already I was controlled by rules and regulations which restricted my desire for joyful abandonment. Governed always by rules, I was a constrained, thoughtful little girl, who grew to be a quiet big girl, who grew to be a reserved, contemplative adult. Yet my mind always remained open to the unknown, to possibilities, to learning.

I loved school. I loved the smell of its chalk, its books and papers. I loved the school library, in which our class spent one mandatory hour each week. I loved the schedule, the order, the quiet, the control of the classroom. I felt safe in school. So much peaceful joy, and to be able to learn, too! Home was poor—small, cramped, disorganized, dingy. Mama had little sense of art and, to my small person, the lack of beauty translated into joylessness. In school there were pretty clippings on the bulletin board, pictures on the walls, colored crayons, chalk, books, a library. In school I was happy.

In the evenings, after her work in the butcher shop, Mama would lie down to rest, and permit me to lie at the foot of her bed. Then she would read the daily serial romance (*de Roman*) to me in Yiddish from *Der Tag*, the Jewish daily newspaper. She became completely absorbed in the love story. And should I perchance miss one day's episode, she never failed to relate it to me the very next day in the utmost detail and with much excitement. I hated those tawdry romances, but felt obliged to listen politely, if impatiently, simply because I needed to share something, anything with her. Furthermore, it was the respectful thing to do. Respect for parents was paramount in my upbringing. This literary experience with my mother enhanced my interest in Yiddish, and later I learned to read it, reveling in Sholom Aleichim's incomparable stories of life in the European *shtetlach*.

Every Sabbath we visited my grandparents. During these obligatory visits, I would invariably take a book from my grandfather's bookcase and read. My parents did not think it strange or interesting that a small child removed herself from play with her young cousins to read books. This was taken most matter of factly. When, a short time later, my Uncle Sam became a doctor and opened his practice in the same apartment in which my grandparents and my Aunt Ella and her family lived, I would often sit in his office and leaf through his medical books. While I did not understand much of what I read, it nevertheless stimulated my desire to be a doctor. But nobody cared and nobody heard.

When I was seven or eight, I became fascinated with reading about the lives and accomplishments of famous scientists. It started when, quite by accident, I stumbled upon a series of pamphlets in the school library entitled *Health Heroes*.

Quite vividly I recall the format of those inspirational

pamphlets. The cover-page was robin's egg blue. In the center of each cover was a small oval cut-out through which one could see the face of a scientist with his or her name below. At the bottom of the page appeared the words "Metropolitan Life Insurance Company." Each pamphlet was devoted to one scientist: Marie Curie, Edward Jenner, Robert Koch, Florence Nightingale, Louis Pasteur, Walter Reed, Edward Livingston Trudeau. Having read and reread each one, I knew my life's goal. I was going to be a doctor or a scientist when I grew up!

I also read Paul de Kruif's *Microbe Hunters* with extreme intensity and excitement. How my emotions overflowed! My eyes filled with tears as I read of Pasteur's successful experiments on bacterial contamination leading to the universal pasteurization of raw milk, and of Lister's remarkable work in antisepsis, identifying unsterile instruments as the source of post-surgical infection in hospitals.

At the same time, I was devouring every Horatio Alger book I could find. If Alger's heroes could come up from their humble poverty-stricken beginnings, couldn't this little Jewish girl from the Bronx ghetto become a great Health Hero like Pasteur or Lister or Madame Curie? I would become a medical microbiologist or a bacteriologist or a medical research doctor and go on to fame and glory, having made the world a safer, better place in which to live.

My maternal grandfather, the Reverend Julius Friedland, was a quiet man who spoke few words. I never knew him to communicate with anybody but my father. Every Sabbath afternoon they would sit at Zaida's dining room table in rapt discussion with one another, two reverends surrounded by open ancient Hebrew tomes, deep in the study of the written words.

Mid-afternoon the two men would break for a cup of hot *tchai*. I can remember Zaida dipping his sugar cube into the teacup, taking a long, loud, lip-smacking suck on the cube, and dipping it once again into the teacup. Nobody dared interrupt these two. They would sit deep in study all afternoon, reading, discussing, quietly disputing until early evening. Then Tante Ella would scurry around to set the table for dinner, and the men were forced to close their books. I may have learned how to study from this pair, how to remove myself from the profane world through books and study.

Although my grandfather made no strong attempt to foster literacy in any of his children or grandchildren, all his offspring, except my mother and her sister Minnie, obtained an American secular education. Jennie and Minnie, the two oldest daughters, had to work in the garment industry, the sweat shops of New York, sewing blouses in order to help support the family. My aunts Ella and Sarah managed to become crackerjack bookkeeper-secretaries. Being women, that was as far as they were permitted to go. Traditionally, marriage was to be their goal. The men, however, went on to college. Uncle Henry graduated from Columbia College as a pharmacist, and Uncle Sam went to Bellevue Medical School and became a doctor, the family hero, protector of the clan. He practiced medicine until well into his eighties, and, as a child, I loved him and wished to emulate him.

If Zaida took any interest in his grandchildren, leastwise in me, I was not aware of it. But I loved his collection of English books and wished so much for him to recognize my zeal for learning, to encourage me to read those books. But that did not happen. When I was ten, I purloined his copy of Voltaire's *Candide* and a beautiful leather-bound copy of Shakespeare's plays (which I still own today, although the leather cover is now shattered with age) and painstakingly read them a bit at a time. It was not until much later when in college that those literary works made much sense to me. But, as a child, I would brag to those who would listen that my grandfather had given me his books to read when I was ten. A wish, but not the truth.

When I was about eleven, Zaida died. He was seventy-two years old. It was not that I loved Zaida so much or that I would miss him, it was rather the sad way life left his body that disturbed me. It was a bright, sunny Saturday morning, almost noon. He had just finished the Sabbath prayers and was walking slowly, ponderously, down Morris Avenue, the few short blocks from the synagogue to his home. Suddenly, without warning he fell.

Morris Avenue was in a densely populated Bronx neighborhood and a crowd of concerned people quickly gathered around him. "Get a doctor!" someone must have shouted. "Get a doctor!" At this precise moment my Uncle Sam, the doctor and family savior, was driving his sleek black Buick down Morris Avenue and saw the crowd. He must have slowed and hesitated for a moment. Should he stop? This was obviously not his business. No, he would drive on. When he later learned that it was his father who had lain on the ground, dead or dying, Uncle Sam was devastated.

That day my uncle failed his father, and he failed me too. I was young and full of the desire to emulate my uncle, to save lives. If I were a doctor, I would have stopped. How could Uncle Sam have ignored his sworn duty to help? What about the Hippocratic oath? What about just plain ethics? The respect and admiration I had for my uncle dropped a notch the day Zaida died.

When Papa failed at his chicken-market enterprise in 1926, he once again purchased a butcher shop, in a different Bronx location on East 176th Street, and we moved from Teller Avenue across town to 1819 Clinton Avenue, one block away from the new store.

This made me very unhappy because I did not like Papa's occupation of butcher. The word butcher connoted to me a *grob-jung*, an uncultured, crude, untutored clod. Papa, by contrast, was a gentle, learned, spiritual man. Throughout my life, I was ashamed to speak of him as a butcher and never did. When asked my father's occupation, I invariably answered, "Reverend." And this is truly who he was, a man worthy of reverence. He had papers to prove it. Some were written in Russian, some in Hebrew, and some in Aramaic, signed by rabbis and dated in the late 1800s. The documents attested to the fact that my father, Yaakov Zvi Bobrov, was a fully qualified person to serve as a *schochet* in any Jewish community and that he had been examined in the laws of *schechita* and had been found to be expert in every aspect. To me, Papa was always a holy man, a learned man, a member of the clergy. In my mind he was *not* a butcher, even when he returned to working in a butcher shop.

But now Mama was taken from me again. She was back full time, flicking chickens and cutting, chopping, and selling meat. I missed being with her. I remember my abhorrence of the lice that Papa and Mama brought home after a day's work. All evening they would sit and scratch their bodies as they talked together or read the Jewish newspaper. There were no showers in the tenements in those days. It was a bath or nothing. Since they were always bone tired during the week, a weekly bath, Erev Shabbat, the night before the Sabbath, was all they permitted themselves. Besides the lice, there was the unpleasant odor of their unwashed bodies.

I, too, had only a weekly bath on Sunday night in preparation for the school week. One day, early in my school career, when the final bell rang, the teacher gave us permission to get our coats from the wardrobe. As I passed one of my classmates, I heard him whisper under his breath, "Gee, you stink." That remark may or may not have been meant for me, but I took it to be for me, and I have never forgotten it. As a result, I am compulsively clean about my person.

Our next apartment at 1819 was infested with ants. They were everyplace. Even the icebox was crawling with them. Mama could not keep food in the house without its being completely overrun.

One day Mama had a brainstorm. In the kitchen was a wooden clothes dryer which hung close to the ceiling and which we pulled up or down by a pulley. It was meant for drying clothes, but Mama decided to use it for food as well. She would put her bread and other perishables on the dryer and hoist the food up close to the ceiling where the ants could not reach it. We didn't stay in that apartment long before we moved a street away to 1879 Clinton Avenue, one block closer to the butcher shop.

Another plague that visited the crowded Bronx tenements was bedbugs. These insects, which infested our beds, resembled small, brown lentils. When squashed, they spurted out a huge drop of red human blood, if they had recently fed. I was disgusted to see, very often, small blood spots on the bedsheets where these bloodsuckers had been crushed by the weight of someone's body.

Every few months Mama would perform a fire ritual. She and I pulled the mattress off the bed and leaned it against the bedroom wall. Then she wrapped newspapers in a cone shape about twenty inches long, as if protecting a bunch of flowers, and lit the torch. Holding it in her hand, she would pass the lighted torch around the springs of the bed. In those days we had no upholstered box springs, so the metal coils were completely exposed. Here, in the crevices of the springs, the bugs lived and bred. I was terrified as I stood by, trembling, watching my mother, torch in hand, attempting to rid our beds of these creatures. I prayed the house would not go up in flames.

All sorts of vermin, bedbugs, ants, lice, cockroaches, and mice lived, hid, and bred in the multitude of apartments of the crowded, dirty tenements. Every month or so an exterminator would appear to spread noxious-smelling powders into the corners of our flat and into the closets. But with fifty or more clean and not so clean families packed into each building, and with many of these buildings on each street, there was no way to control the vermin.

Each year of my young life I hated the dirty, ugly, crowded Bronx more and continued to plead with my parents to liberate our family from the city. "Papa," I would say, "you are a reverend, a *schochet*, a *mohel*, a *malamed*. You can make a living anyplace where even a few Jews live. You are smart and educated. You could teach children Yiddish and Hebrew, kill chickens and cows in accordance with the laws of *kashrut*, give sermons in the synagogue. Let's move to the country."

My brother would add his pleas to mine. But our words fell on deaf ears. It was impossible to move our parents from their comfort zone, the New York City ghetto and its multitude of Jews. Solly and I soon understood we would have to wait until we could earn our own living before we could leave New York City.

Some few memories of my life from the third through the fifth grades remain with me, still vivid.

Miss McMurray, my fourth grade teacher, was a tall gentile woman in charge of a class of ragtag Jewish ghetto kids. Christmas in her class was big confusion for me. She had had delivered into our classroom a huge Christmas tree which reached to the ceiling. We pupils were directed to help her decorate the tree with multicolored glass baubles and angels, ornaments and trinkets, the likes of which I had never before seen. The colors, shapes, and designs dazzled me. And above all, at the very top of the tree, she placed a large luminous white star. It was not the six-pointed star of David, the *Mogen David*, which I knew. It was a five-pointed star. Why was it missing a sixth point? She did not explain this. She led us in singing Christmas songs. In my childish imagination, yearning for some beauty in my drab life, I could see white snow falling in a rural countryside far away from the filth of the New York City streets, a horse-drawn sleigh, stars twinkling brightly in the pristine night sky, the air smelling clean and crisp, snapping cold. And we kids sang loud and off key, "Jingle bells, jingle bells, jingle all the way, oh, what fun it is to ride in a one-horse open sleigh-eh." And although it was really a Thanksgiving song rather than truly a Christmas song, we sang "Over the river and through the woods, to Grandmother's house we go. The horse knows the way to carry the sleigh through the white and drifting snow-oh."

But what of the religious connotations of the songs we were singing? Therein lay the confusion! Miss McMurray had us sing songs like "Away in a Manger" and "Joy to the World" and "Oh, Come, All Ye Faithful." I remember words like "Christ our Lord was born on Christmas day," words I could not, dared not, utter, let alone sing joyfully. I faked it. I opened my mouth but my lips could not declare the glory of Christ. It hurt me that I could not, dared not, partake of her joy in Christ and Christmas. It was difficult for a child of my strict Orthodox Jewish background to celebrate the birth of Jesus. It set up great conflict in me. It contradicted what I had been taught from birth.

The day before Christmas recess, Miss McMurray handed each of us a little bag of candy, crystallized sugar cubes in which were embedded enchanting floral images which to my childish eyes appeared like beautiful antique millifiore. They were so colorful and captivating I did not want to suck on them and see the flowers grow dim as they dissolved and disappeared. I took the little bag of candy home. Nobody was there. No tree, no singing, no joy. So, all alone, I sang "Jingle Bells," but not the other songs which extolled Christ—no, not those. And I dreamed of a beautiful snow-covered landscape and the joy of a beautiful holiday I dared not celebrate.

On that same day I was obliged to bring a Christmas present to Miss McMurray. It was an unspoken rule: every child in that class knew he or she must bring a present for teacher, although we were all, to a person, Jews.

Mama acceded to my demand, although money was scarce. She and I went down the hill to the corner drugstore owned by Mr. Pryluck, the pharmacist, who was also a Jew. Of course he was a Jew; this was, after all, *our* ghetto. There she purchased a matching set of cologne and talcum powder, which Mr. Pryluck wrapped for us in colorful Christmas paper. I delivered the gift to school the next day. I had never received nor given presents on Chanukah, which was *our* holiday. It wasn't done in those days. But the idea of presents fascinated me. Christians seemed to have such fun on their holiday. Jews, like my parents and me, had only hard work around that time of year, filling meat and chicken orders, delivering them to customers. Why couldn't we Jews have happy, colorful holidays?

Chanukah, in my childhood, was actually considered a minor holiday, not worthy of much celebration. On the Sunday that fell somewhere between the eight days of Chanukah, all my family, aunts, uncles, and cousins, gathered at the home of my grandparents. One or another of my aunts would light the menorah, the *chanukia*, cover her face with her hands and hastily mumble a few prayers in Hebrew. No one bothered to translate the Hebrew words into Yiddish or English so we kids could understand. Nor did anyone attempt to explain the significance of the holiday. Nor did we understand why it was traditional to eat potato latkes at that time of year. Nor why the menorah was lighted each night for eight nights. Our drab holiday could not substitute for the glitter, the color, the joyousness of Christmas. Even the candles on the menorah were a dull, monotone orange. It wasn't until years later that Jews began to light multicolored Chanukah candles, probably in an attempt to emulate the colors of Christmas, to make our Chanukah holiday somewhat more attractive to Jewish children. I was happy to see the drab orange go, but colored candles alone did little to enhance the Chanukah experience.

At Chanukah each year, the family would gather around the dining room table at my grandparents' house, eat potato latkes hot off the griddle in massive amounts, and kibitz around. There were no presents, no decorations, no particular pride in our heritage. There was only tradition and the sociability of an unexciting, mundane family gathering. After latkes, the male adults would walk around the table, one at a time, handing each kid a quarter or a half-dollar, Chanukah *gelt*. By day's end, each of us had collected a few dollars and, with our "catch" and a belly full of potato latkes, we departed for home. No great joy. No colorfully wrapped presents. No "Jingle Bells." No songs. At home, I handed the money over to my mother, who, the following day, carried it to the Dollar Savings Bank. Even had I dared request a toy or a book be purchased with the money, it would not have happened. In my family the rule was: "This money goes to the bank so you can go to college when you grow up."

At the end of the sixth grade, when I was eleven, my parents were notified that I was being transferred to Herman Ridder Junior High School #98 at the other side of Crotona Park. The brighter children in the class were being transferred, provided their parents agreed to it. The rest would remain at P.S. 44 to finish the seventh and eighth grades and then go on to high school as freshmen.

Junior high school meant accelerated studies for three years, at the end of which time we would enter high school as sophomores. Transfer to junior high also meant a long walk of some two miles forth and back through a lonely, deserted park.

My parents did not consult me as to what I preferred. On the one hand, I did not want to leave my classmates behind. Also I did not want to lose the comfortable proximity to a school to which I had grown accustomed after five years. On the other hand, I might have been wise enough to know I must make the move for my academic growth. After all, school was my only validation, my only success so far. If the powers that be said I was bright and should be transferred, did I have a choice? My grades were excellent, and I understood the suggested transfer represented a present equal to Miss Shields' pencil box. Most of my friends stayed on in P.S. 44. I moved to Herman Ridder Junior High #98.

And yet again we moved, this time one block away to 1879 Clinton Avenue, to an apartment in a well-kept, small brownstone. Small apartment houses such as this one were an exception in the Bronx. Only three families lived here, one on each of the three floors. We lived on the middle floor. For the first time in my eleven years of life, I did not have to share a bedroom with my brother. This was pure joy. I walked to school each day, across Crotona Park to Herman Ridder Junior High School, in sun, in rain, in snow, a very long walk through the lonely, deserted park.

To furnish my first very own bedroom, my parents took me to a secondhand furniture store on Third Avenue. There I was permitted to pick out a cheap dresser, a twin-sized bed, and a desk. The desk cost two dollars, and I was very proud of it. It wasn't really a desk. It was a narrow table with Queen Anne legs, about fifteen inches wide and a yard long. It was not really large enough for my books when they were open, but adequate if I were to open only one book at a time. This pseudo-desk served through my entire educational career until I graduated from Columbia.

For a nightstand, I used Mama's Singer sewing machine. It did not look like a sewing machine when it was closed, but rather like an over-sized, square oak box with a raised laurel leaf decoration on its face. On it I placed bookends, white glazed ceramic Indian heads, factory seconds, cheap because the glaze was marred by little raised speckles. It made no matter to me. The bookends were mine, and they brought me joy. Between the bookends I would place the few books I was currently reading. These would change weekly.

Each Sunday, in rain, in snow, in the cold chill of early morning winter or the sweltering, humid heat of summer, I walked the two-plus miles to the public library. By eight o'clock when the library doors sprang open, a line had already formed—a line of first-generation American kids, eager to read. I invariably arrived early so as to be close to the head of the line. First in line (or as close as I could come to it) meant the best choice of books—a mystery, a romantic novel of Colonial America, a book of plays, a story about a scientist. I had my favorites, and I knew the exact shelves on which to find them.

My bedroom was a small room with a large closet running the length of one wall. At my request for something pretty, Mama trimmed my white pullback dotted Swiss curtains with blue ribbon. The single window faced out on an alley, as did a multitude of windows from neighboring, close-in apartment houses. Not much light could enter.

Ours was a long railroad apartment. It was necessary to walk through each room to get to the next, except for my parents' bedroom, which was at the head of the apartment, windows facing the street. Except for this room, one walked down a long hallway, through my bedroom, through the dining room, through the kitchen, ending in my brother's room, where the window exited onto a fire escape.

On Friday afternoons it was my responsibility to tidy up the house in preparation for the Sabbath. As soon as I came home from school, I began work. I would change the beds and put the dirty linens in the wash tub. By this time Mama would have arrived from the butcher shop, and we would start preparing food for the Sabbath. Time permitting, Mama would bake a *challah* and I, perhaps, a simple cake. These preparations over, I washed the kitchen floor with a scrub brush and spread newspaper over it to keep it clean until Papa and Solly arrived. As the sun began to set, we were ready to sit down to our Sabbath meal.

It is Erev Shabbat, the peaceful night before the Sabbath. I spread a sparkling white damask cloth on the kitchen table and place the four gleaming silver candlesticks in the middle. Mama pours the traditional sweet sacramental wine into a silver Kiddush cup. She lights the candles and, covering her face with her hands, prays in Hebrew hurriedly, inaudibly, "Blessed is the Lord our God, Ruler of the universe, who hallows us with mitzvot *and commands us to kindle the lights of Shabbat." Papa lifts his silver* becher (cup) *high and recites the Kiddush in the ancient traditional sing-song. Now he cuts off the heel of the* challah *and hands each of us a piece of* bread. *Blessings proclaimed, our home is filled with quiet joy as we gratefully acknowledge the presence of God in our midst.*

The Friday night meal was always sweet and dear to me. It was the only time during the busy week when all the family dined together and peace and quiet reigned. Papa spoke of it as *shalom beit*, peace in the home. On Erev Shabbat, the family had time to talk, to listen, to discuss, to dream, to simply be together and enjoy one another's company. It was during one of these Erev Shabbat meals that I gave Papa a lesson in evolution, a subject about which he knew nothing. Naturally, evolution was not one of the subjects he had studied in the Russian *yeshiva*.

That day we had been having a discussion on evolution in biology class in junior high. My science teacher, Mr. Schleifer, was fresh out of college and hot on the subject. Biology fascinated me. So did tall, good-looking Mr. Schleifer, who had a way of winking at me whenever he passed me in the hall. Ah, young budding love! That Friday in class, he was discussing the sturgeon as an example of the evolutionary process. He told us that evolution was a process by which certain structures, through time, become modified in order to better protect the species from extinction.

The word sturgeon elicited gustatory excitement in me, my salivary juices flowed. For years I had yearned to taste this fish. Smoked, neatly sliced, and tantalizingly displayed, it lay in the showcase of the Jewish deli whenever I went there to shop with Mama. But Papa forbade it in our house. "It is *traif*," he said. "It is a fish which has no scales, so it's the same as shrimp, or clams or oysters, all dirty, *traif*, not kosher. Jews do not eat things like that."

But now I sensed that evolutionary truth might set us free! Mr. Schleifer explained that the sturgeon is a true fish belonging to the order Pisces.

"The fish as we know it today," Mr. Schleifer said, "has

true scales, but only in its embryonic form. Thousands of years ago, the mature sturgeon had scales *throughout* its life, but after generations of evolving, the scales now appear only in the fish's embryonic stage and are later lost. By the time the fish reaches maturity, the scales are replaced by rigid, impenetrable plates arranged along the fish's back and sides, plates which protect it from being devoured by its enemies. Thus, by modification of the scales to form plates, the species has been able to survive through millennia."

This story, in simple words, I relayed to Papa at the dinner table that Erev Shabbat. Papa listened attentively. He was not a closed-minded religionist. True, he believed God had created the universe and everything in it in six days, but perhaps God was still at work modifying, correcting, perfecting his early handiwork. Papa cogitated silently for a few moments.

"This is very interesting," he said. Then, "*Nu,* so sturgeon is *glat kosher!*" Papa had put his *hechsher,* his stamp of approval, on the fish.

Now that sturgeon had evolved from *traif* to kosher, Mama bought a small piece at the deli. The smoked flesh of this large, sharp-snouted fish was a delicacy, so good! And kosher. But, oh, how expensive!

While living at 1879, late Friday afternoon, if time permitted after chores, I would crawl onto my bed to read the *Ladies' Home Journal.* Like other young boys his age, my brother, Solly, had been recruited to sell magazines door to door. Usually it was the families of those boys that ended up buying the magazines. Mama had been talked into taking a subscription. The neat, beautiful home that I did not live in, the sweet savory non-kosher recipes that were not cooked in my home, all these I found in the *Ladies' Home Journal.* It arrived on Fridays once a month. How I looked forward to the beautiful pictures of rooms in lovely homes, of delicious colorful recipes, of lovely fashionable clothes, of flowering gardens. I yearned to escape the dingy ghetto. Woman's rightful place is in the home (a beautiful, well-organized one), the magazine proclaimed. And I believed it. Well, almost.

Once a week, I did the family wash on a glass scrubbing board in the kitchen washtub. I would then climb through the window in Solly's room, onto the fire escape, and hang the clothes on the clothesline, a sturdy cord which stretched for many yards from a pulley outside our window to a large pole some distance away. Afraid of falling, I tried never to look down. Down was two stories and certain death. On days when the temperature dropped to freezing and below, the clothes would become hard and stiff, and it was especially difficult for a small girl to reel them in.

While hanging clothes, I would often hear the rag-pickers in the back yard chanting, "I cash clo-thes, I cash clo-thes" in sing-song. Often a poor beggar would sing a ditty or strum a banjo or scrape on a violin. I would throw a penny down. In those days of bitter poverty, even a penny could buy something. It was the late 1920s, early 1930s.

I was very happy to have my very own bedroom, but, sadly, for reasons not divulged to me, we moved again, this time to 764 East 176th Street, and again I was deprived of my privacy. Once again I was forced to share a bedroom with Solly.

Solly bullied and belittled me, and I, five years younger than he, was not physically or verbally agile enough to defend myself.

"I'll betcha I'm smarter than you," I would often scream in frustration, something I did not really believe.

"Betcha? Betcha? What kind of English is that, you dummy. Spell it," he confronted me one day.

"Betcha. B-E-T-C-H-A."

"No, stupid, it is two words—*bet you*."

Still, I fought back hard.

"I'll betcha a penny I'm right," I whimpered, unwilling to acknowledge defeat. But I knew Solly was right. I always came up second best.

The new two-bedroom apartment was located on the same street as the butcher shop, just down a bit. Across the street was P.S. 44, where I had attended school from the time I was seven until I was eleven.

I disliked this new apartment. The room I shared with Solly was plain and ugly, furnished only with twin beds and a huge rolltop desk. I will never know where my parents obtained this old hulk. It was ancient, scarred, and battle-weary. But it was also full of wonderment, for it contained a million little cubicles, cubbyholes, and drawers, none of which had ever been completely emptied by its former owner, whoever that might have been. And each drawer and cubbyhole held yet another surprise: clips, small pads of paper, large pads, loose sheets of various colored paper, adding machine tapes, bill forms. I had such fun playing at that desk. I used it only for play, never for study. Sitting at the huge desk, I could imagine I was any big shot I wished to be. For the serious matter of study I still used my two-dollar Queen-Ann-legged psuedo-desk, now residing in the small, dark foyer of our new apartment. My parents disposed of the rolltop desk when we moved again. Just as I do not know how it came to us, I do not know where it went.

When we moved to 176th Street, Solly was about sixteen and had already begun to date. When he had coed parties, always on a Saturday night when my parents were at work, he would shove me into the bedroom, slamming the door tight.

"Don't leave the bedroom, fat horse," he would threaten. "I'll beat you up if you come out."

Relegated to the back bedroom, I could hear laughter emanating from the forbidden room. I was sad, certain I was indeed the ugly, fat horse Solly so often told me I was. Was that why I had to stay in the bedroom alone?

To add insult to injury, on weekdays after school it became my responsibility to prepare the supper meal. If I failed to do this, there might be no meal that evening.

My mother decided that chicken was the easiest thing for a child to cook. By the time I arrived from school to the store, she had already cut up and koshered the chicken. This meant she had sprinkled it heavily with coarse salt, and then, after a while, soaked it in water to remove the salt and any traces of remaining blood. Jews are not permitted to consume blood.

If I cooked the chicken in the store, I would bring a pot down from the apartment, wash the chicken, cover it with water, throw in a whole peeled onion, and put it up to cook in the lice-infested back room where Mama and Papa plucked chickens. This meant I had to wade through lice-infested feathers, ankle-deep, to get to the little two-burner gas stove. My alternative was to take the pot and chicken upstairs to the apartment and cook it there. In either case, I had to face the fright of striking a match, fearing the gas might explode in my face. To this day I do not eat boiled chicken.

I was a shy child, quiet, obedient. I rarely answered back to my parents or to any authority figure. If I raised my voice to my mother, Papa would sternly, though gently, reprimand me for lacking respect. I never threw a tantrum. Rarely would I cry, except when Solly hit me, which he did often. Then I would complain bitterly to my mother, with little relief or comfort from her. She always seemed to champion Solly's cause. Was this because boys were more important than girls? It was a difficult journey I made through my early childhood, but in spite of all our bickering, I learned later that my brother and I truly loved one another, although this was not apparent to either of us in our early years. And when we learned it, it was already too late. As for being a girl who did not *deserve* support, well, I never did work that issue out with my mother.

Often my mother would brag about my scholastic ability when she met her cronies on the street. "Ruthie always comes home from school and says she failed but she always gets A's." This public announcement always caused me to cringe in embarrassment and anger. My stomach would knot up; I had the wish to flee.

First of all, her boasting embarrassed me. It was not true that I always got A's—although I got many. My anger, however, was something different. In the privacy of home, she often said, "Why is it Solly never needs to study? He can go to school easy without working hard like you." What I heard in my head was, "You, Ruthie, are a stupid girl. Solly is smart. He can get good grades hands down." In actuality, Solly barely squeaked through school. He was bright, but not studious. When it came time for him to enter college, he was held back until he had completed several outstanding high school requirements. What Mother said about me in private contradicted what she said in public, and her duplicity angered me. Whether she was aware of it or not, she was constantly pitting me against my brother. My brother, the male, was brighter than I, a mere female. Mama set the stage early for what I would encounter throughout the rest of my life.

Early Adolescence with a Few Backward Glances _____

When I was twelve, I began to explore the boundaries beyond the Bronx. I would often take a Saturday trip downtown to Manhattan to the Museum of Art or the Museum of Natural History. Of all my studies, I loved biology and art the most. Those trips always involved a long, up- and downhill walk to and from the subway, and I always made these trips alone. My parents, from their totally different background, did not partake of these kinds of intellectual pursuits. They did not hinder me, but neither did they encourage me.

Sometimes I would go to the Metropolitan Opera. For fifty cents, I could stand in the back of the orchestra section amidst a crowd of people huddled close together, the strong smell of garlic permeating the air. Although I was a tall child, it was difficult for me to see from the back of the hall and over the heads of so many adults.

Sometimes when I was downtown, I would step into a bookstore to browse. There were no bookstores that I was aware of in the Bronx, none in my vicinity at least. If I had a few extra coins and came across an interesting, inexpensive book, I would buy it. Perhaps a small copy of *The Rubayat, The Family Moscat, Parnassus on Wheels*, a book of poetry. Invariably when I returned home, Mama would scold me. "Why are you buying books? There are libraries, no? Soon I will throw you out of the house with all your books!" It was Mama's persistent harping "no books" that has, in large part, made me the inveterate compulsive book collector that I am.

My Hebrew education started when I was nine. I attended secular school at P.S. 44 until 3 P.M. After that came Hebrew school called *chaider* or *Talmud Torah*. I hated going. I needed the time to do my secular school homework and to take a break from a long day's work. Instead I was faced with two hours of *chaider* each late afternoon except Friday and Saturday. After *chaider* there was homework for both public school and religious school. And, as if that were not enough, on Sunday when I wanted to read the funny papers, listen to the radio, or relax a bit, I had to attend Hebrew classes all morning. That gave me very little time to myself except for the Sabbath.

Hebrew school was usually an appendage to a synagogue. Usually it was upstairs from the House of Worship (*Beth Hamidrash*) or downstairs in the basement, depending upon available space in the building which housed the *schul*. My parents paid for my religious education; it was not gratis.

There were a great number of self-declared *melamdim* (Hebrew teachers) in New York City in my day. Almost any immigrant Jew with a little knowledge of Bible, Hebrew grammar, or Talmud (obtained in a European *yeshiva*) could hire himself out to teach. In most instances, he knew barely enough English to communicate with his American students; he spoke only Yiddish. But most American kids did not understand Yiddish as well as I. Furthermore, these self-styled teachers had no concept of how to teach. So chaos reigned in the *chaider*. I would have enjoyed studying Hebrew in a proper setting, but, as it was, I felt *chaider* to be an unnecessary burden.

Ignoring my complaints, my parents insisted I attend. I found every excuse to skip class. I would invent bellyaches and toothaches, or protest it was too cold or raining too hard to venture outdoors. In spite of my excuses, go I must! One terrifying incident saved me from Hebrew school, at least from that particular one, although it left an indelible mark on my psyche and could have cost me my life.

By the age of twelve I had already been attending *chaider* for three years. The walk from home to the synagogue was approximately a mile. The streets were already dark at 6 P.M. when I had to leave the house. It was a bitter cold, dark night, and few people were about. Snow had just begun to fall and dust the streets with a soft white cover. As I crossed Tremont Avenue, which was brightly lit because of the many shops, I came into a dark street about three blocks from the school. Snow was falling rapidly now and in a few minutes had already laid a two-inch cover on the ground. Suddenly I became aware of footsteps behind me. They were muffled but seemed to be getting closer. I saw nobody on the street, but, as I turned my head, I glimpsed the dark outline of a man behind me, shoulders hunched under a huge black coat. With growing terror, I walked faster and faster, yet he was gaining on me. As he came close, I heard him mutter sinister sounds under his breath.

And then I heard his words, "I'm going to fork you between your legs," he said in a low, gruff, menacing voice.

I did not understand what "fork" meant, but from his tone I knew he meant me harm. I took off like a shot, running. I made the three long blocks to the synagogue in record time, pulled open the heavy door, and fell breathless into the brightness and warmth of the school vestibule. I leaned against the door, my heart pounding, my body quivering.

That night I learned even less Hebrew than usual. All I could think about was how I was going to get home. What if he was still waiting for me outside the building? What if, when I came through the door, he grabbed me and strangled me? Should I call my parents? My brother? I should have, but I did not. I was already in the habit of taking care of myself, even when I really needed help.

Class over, I started out of school walking with a classmate until Tremont Avenue, where he turned off. While I was in the well-lighted street and with a partner, I was not too fearful, but now I had two more blocks of darkness to go alone.

What now? The man had not yet appeared. I kept going, my heart pounding heavily, running all the way. The streets were deserted, the snow was still falling, and I knew any footsteps would be completely soundless in the deepening snow. I got to my apartment building, opened the door into the vestibule, and dashed up the stairs.

My mother and father were already in bed, their bedroom door closed. I knocked on the door.

"*Kum arein,*" my mother called.

I could hardly breathe. Sitting on the side of her bed, I poured out my terrifying story. And by then I clearly understood what the man had meant for me. It was dangerous and threatening to be a girl.

The next day my mother did not insist I return to that particular *chaider.* Instead, she took me to a small house around the corner from home, a small house which had been converted into a house of worship. In the basement, which consisted of one large room, school was held. I would not have a long walk, just out the apartment building and around the corner. "See, just like being at home," Mama said. But there was nothing to learn there. The teacher, an old European rabbi, knew no English. He struggled mightily to translate Genesis from Hebrew into a mixture of English and Yiddish, "Yinglish," as Leo Rosten calls it. Recognizing me as an apt student, he gave me his job:

"*Nu, maidele, du vertaitsh.* Please, take the class," he said to me in Yiddish. With that he disappeared out the door. We saw him only sporadically from then on until the end of the semester.

For the next two years until, with great effort and much pleading, I finally convinced my parents they were wasting their money and my time, I learned little Hebrew. And here my formal Hebrew education ended, though not my interest in Judaism.

One summer day I was wearing a thin dress against the

unrelenting heat. My young breasts were just beginning to develop. Mother knew nothing about training bras, so my little tits were unprotected, sticking innocently through the sheer fabric like large pimples. Business was slow at the butcher shop this hot day. On such days, Mama would often take a chair outside to sit and read the Yiddish newspaper between tending customers. Or a neighbor lady might join her and they would sit together and chat. On this day, an old lady sat with her as I approached. I asked Mother's permission to take a few pennies from the cash register to buy a cold drink at the candy store next door.

As I stood there, the old lady reached out and touched my tiny breasts, first one, then the other. I instinctively drew back, assaulted. *Mother, I thought, say something to this old hag. Protect me.* Instead Mama laughed embarrassedly. She had not a glimmer of understanding of my humiliation. With repugnance, I remember the gleeful, lascivious look on the old lady's face as her hand touched my sensitive young body. What was she thinking?

Time passed and I continued to grow and develop sexually. But my concept of myself as an attractive female did not. I desperately needed a proper role model, a woman happy with her own femininity, to teach me about myself. No such person was in sight. Mother was cold, powerful, certainly more powerful than my father, almost the antithesis of what I envisioned feminine might be. And she showed no interest in cosmetics or jewelry or things usually associated with femininity. Nor was there any female in my family whom I wished to emulate.

Movie heroines in the 1920s and '30s were no help either. I could never hope to achieve their immaculate perfection. Furthermore, it seemed their one aim in life was to "get a man." If, on occasion, a professional woman was depicted in a film, a doctor or a lawyer, she was not successful unless and until she had "hooked" her man. Then, invariably, having achieved this life goal, she would relinquish her profession to full-time domesticity. It seemed the need to possess a man was the center of woman's universe. Was a woman really nothing without a man? Part of me bought the hype, part of me rebelled. I was confused. Which way does a woman go to be happy and successful—the way indicated by her parents, by society, by the movies...or the way she truly would like to go if only she dared to go against the tide?

At twelve I began to menstruate. Although Mother assured me this event was normal, I was still frightened. "However," she cautioned me, "be very careful from now on. You can easily become pregnant."

"Will I become pregnant if I stand close to a boy or if he touches me?" I asked innocently in ignorance.

"No," she answered. At that point, she told me about intercourse.

She said that when a man and a woman were married, they were permitted to sleep together in the same bed, not necessarily in twin beds like in the movies. When they held one another close, the man's penis would become large and hard and red and he would insert this into the woman's vagina. Such behavior was permitted only for married people. Never, never was it permitted if the persons were not married to one another.

I was shocked, incredulous. I did not want to accept what she said. I could not believe that my sweet, loving father could act in such a repugnant manner. She omitted any mention of love. I was left with the sense that intercourse was a unilateral act of male aggression which brought pleasure only to the male partner.

I knew my mother was devoted to my father by virtue of her *ketubah*, her holy marriage vows. The fact that she had had two children by him in that ugly, bizarre way proved her devotion. But what about love? She did not speak of love or of pleasure for herself. Certainly she did not speak of passion. I never saw her kiss Papa or even stroke him affectionately. Occasionally I would see Papa hug her spontaneously. He always instigated the action, never she. And when he hugged her, his hand would invariably go to her breast. Beyond that, I was not aware of any overt act of sexual love between them.

For a long while following this unpleasant discussion with my mother, I found it difficult to look Papa full in the face. However, my childhood love for him never diminished. I think I dismissed everything Mama had said. Her description of intercourse left me disbelieving, afraid of men, disgusted, embarrassed, and very confused. Yet, in some incomprehensible way, I seemed to be attracted to boys.

Papa was a religious man. As such, I knew it was improper for him to openly display his warm sexual feelings in public. Even for a husband to hold his wife's hand in public was frowned upon by Orthodox Jews. However, Papa and Mama walked arm in arm on the Sabbath. The ancient custom of the wife walking six steps behind her husband was not practiced in our family. Propriety and decorum were. So I continued to find it difficult to understand sexual intimacy.

Papa once related a story to me, probably in defense of his own sexuality. Many years ago, he said, in a *shtetl* in Europe, two temple elders had occasion to visit the rabbi's modest one-room cottage (*stible*) on an early morning and, seeing the bed in disarray, one said to the other: "*Oy, ze nur. Is dos nisht a shande?* (Look at that. Isn't that shame?)," implying that the bed was rumpled because the rabbi had probably had intercourse with his wife the night before. To which the other Jew answered: "*Nu, denkst du as de rebbe's neshume is a ruzinke?* (Well, do you think the rabbi's soul is merely a raisin?)"

In the Brook Avenue apartment where I was born, there were two bedrooms. One was for my parents, and the other, a tiny windowless room off the kitchen, held one bed which Solly and I shared. However, when we moved to Teller Avenue, the new apartment had only one bedroom, which belonged to my parents. I, six years old at the time, slept in the full-sized bed with them. Solly slept on a small daybed in the dining room. Sometimes, in the night, I would feel the bed shake. So, I thought Papa must be getting ready to go to work, sitting on the edge of the bed, putting on his shoes. I had no knowledge of the hour, nor did I even open my eyes. If I had opened my eyes to see, I might have known it was still dark outside, that it was not yet time for him to go to work, that he was not sitting on the edge of the bed putting on his shoes. I would have understood what I was not yet ready to accept, that the bed sheets might be rumpled in the morning.

I spent three years, from 1930 to 1932, at Herman Ridder Junior High School. There I made two new Jewish friends, both immigrants, Rebecca Gelman, who had just come from Russia, and Lillian Baral, newly arrived from Poland. They were very bright. In spite of their limited knowledge of English, they did well in their classes. The three of us formed a close-knit circle. Our classmates called us The Three Musketeers. I was of help to them with their English, and they were far ahead of me in math and foreign languages.

The principal of Herman Ridder Junior High School was an academic fanatic or, more properly, an educational reformer, leaning heavily to the right. In the depths of the Great Depression, he believed that all children should dress alike so that no one could be singled out as richer or poorer than another. And he had an excellent point, because we were indeed a heterogeneous mixture, children of poor, low-income, middle-class, and wealthy families all attending the same public school. Girls were ordered to wear white blouses and navy-blue skirts; boys, white shirts and navy-blue trousers, a sort of uniform.

I always loved English class. In the last semester at junior high school we were studying Greek mythology. It was a toss-up between Alfred Pelzig and me as to who was going to win the medal for best English student. The runner-up prize was a pin.

On final exam day, I was very nervous. With all my heart I wanted to win the medal, but Alfred beat me out. He came in first, and I a very close second. He won the medal, I the pin. It was a great disappointment for me. Respect for myself was closely tied to my academic acumen. Alfred had done me in. Adding insult to injury, later, after college, he went on to medical school while I, because of my gender, was not permitted the same privilege.

Mr. Schleifer, my science teacher, reminded me of Ichabod Crane. He was the first teacher in my young life on whom I had a crush. He was young, very tall, and very lean. I cannot judge his ability as a scientist, but I won three pins for excellence in his courses. The science pin was smaller than the English pin, about a quarter of an inch long, showing a picture of a wide-eyed owl, below which read BIOLOGY in bold, black letters. I also won several pins for overall academic achievement, one each year.

I disliked Mr. Shimberg, my geometry teacher. From him I learned a strong negative pedagogic lesson: to teach successfully, a teacher must feel compassion for his student, must be an inspiration, a role model. Mr. Shimberg was an information-dispenser; he might as well have been a machine. Furthermore, he lacked any trace of humility.

Each week on Friday we were tested. My Russian friend, Rebecca, and I sat side by side in class. While she may have had a poor knowledge of English, she was outstanding in mathematics. She told me that in Russia in the 1920s all children were tested for innate aptitudes at a very young age. She had scored very high in mathematics and, consequently, her parents were paid a stipend while she attended school. The Russian government promised to train her through college as a mathematician and then place her in a secure government job. I thought this an excellent concept which made the best use of one's natural abilities.

But on this particular Friday, I was in big trouble. Mr. Shimberg passed out his exam. Rebecca dove in, her pencil scratching across her page with lightening speed. The sound paralyzed me. I could not think. I could not write. The thought of trying to compete with this Russian math giant overpowered me. When I finally put pencil to paper, after what seemed an interminable length of time, not much time was left. I finished only a very small portion of the exam. I received a grade of 47 percent.

Humiliated, I approached Mr. Shimberg and explained what had happened, how paralyzed I had been and why. It was Friday afternoon. He handed me another typewritten exam which he folded carefully, put in an envelope, and licked closed. He said: "Take this home and allow yourself exactly fifty minutes. Do this exam by yourself. Do not accept help from anyone and do not consult any books." With those admonitions, he sent me off for the weekend. I was to hand him my paper on Monday morning.

On Friday afternoon, upon arriving home, I had the usual pre-Sabbath chores to perform. No time to take the exam then. Or the next day either. It was forbidden to write on the Sabbath. I could barely wait for the sun to set on Saturday so I could begin my exam. My parents left for the butcher shop following the Havdalah prayers. Solly was off with his friends. I was alone. I set the alarm for fifty minutes and started to write.

In the quiet of my own home, I was easily able to finish in less than the allotted fifty minutes. And I was scrupulously honest. I consulted no person and no book.

Monday morning I delivered my paper to Mr. Shimberg. He graded it on the spot. I made a grade of 98 percent.

"Well," he said, "Let's see. You made 47 on the first, 98 on the second, so we'll average them together...98, 47, OK, that gives you 73 percent."

I was devastated. I knew myself to be an "A" geometry student, perhaps not a genius like Rebecca, but pretty good. It was not fair. I had worked hard, but Mr. Shimberg held all the cards. He made the rules. There was nothing I could do.

On the other hand, I suppose he could have denied me even the second chance.

In New York State, all high school students in every city and hamlet were required to take the very same exam called a Regents exam. This was given in all major subjects. Thousands of students throughout the state of New York took the same exam at exactly the same time. Thus, the State Board of Education could track how well each school throughout the state was performing. When geometry Regents time came, every student in New York State who had studied the subject for one year sat down at the exact hour to take the same test. The exams had been sealed until that moment. Three hours were allotted for it.

Though excited, I knew that three hours would give me ample time to finish, even if I freaked out a bit. When the grades came in, I had received the highest score in the State of New York, even higher than Rebecca's. In fact, that year, the Regents exam was declared beyond the level of high school students, and all grades were automatically "upped" by several points. Except mine. I was already too close to the top. Raising my grade would have brought me above 100 percent. While I felt happy to have proven to Mr. Shimberg, to my classmates, and especially to myself that I was, in fact, an excellent math student, Mr. Shimberg said not a word of praise.

Graduation from junior high school was memorable only for the way we were expected to dress. Even on this auspicious occasion, dress code called for "white blouse and navy-blue skirt for girls; white shirt and navy-blue trousers for boys." Plain and equal. I yearned for something fancier for this occasion. So mother sewed me a new skirt. The skirt was plain dark-blue rayon but, yielding to my wish for something special, the bottom six inches were pleated. The principal could not complain about that. At least I was unique, even if only in the last six inches of my skirt.

Our dingy east Bronx neighborhood was dotted with tenements. As soon as one apartment needed paint, we simply moved to another. Moving was easier than having an apartment painted while we still occupied it. For one thing, the paint and turpentine odors were unbearable; paint took days and even weeks to dry in those days. Another apartment close by was usually easy to find, and it would have been freshly painted before we moved in. One apartment was as good or as bad as another, so we moved many times in my young life. There was no pride of ownership; we always rented.

I was fifteen when we moved across the street to 1879 Prospect Avenue, into a three-room flat. There was one bedroom for my parents, a kitchen, a bathroom, and a dining room. There was also a small dark foyer. By this time, the family had grown somewhat smaller because Solly had gone off to dental school at the University of Buffalo in upstate New York, and I, just about ready to enter college, did not, I suppose, warrant a bedroom.

When we first moved into this apartment, I slept on a studio couch which stood against the right-hand wall of the dining room. Ordinarily we had our meals in the tiny kitchen except on those rare occasions when we had company. And then we used the dining room.

The dining room was also my study room. When I studied there, the large, heavy-limbed table, which dominated the center of the room, became my desk. On arriving home from school, I would carefully lift the lamp that sat in the center of the table and place it on the buffet. The lamp was a cheap pot-metal figure of a flat-chested nude woman in a supine position holding in one hand (an impossible feat considering her size) a large, mottled red, orange, and white globe about six inches round. There was no electrical outlet available at the table, so the lamp had never been lighted. It was strictly decorative in an ugly, useless way.

I would carefully place the lamp on the buffet which stood against the opposite wall from the studio couch and then remove and fold up the cheap tablecloth, with its blue and purple peacocks machine-embroidered on a thin muslin field, trimmed with cheap machine-made lace. My father had bought both these beauties, the lamp and tablecloth, for an undisclosed amount of money when he was downtown on some business or other. He ventured very infrequently from where we lived in the Bronx into sophisticated New York, around Broadway and 42nd Street. Had he gone more frequently, who knows how many more of these *tsatskes* (trinkets) he might have purchased from some thieving street peddler.

I remember the day he brought these items home and fondly presented them to my mother. She took one quick look and roundly chastised him, not particularly for his bad taste, but for spending hard-earned money on junk. However, she never had the courage to toss these things into the garbage. So she resignedly shook her head back and forth in disbelief at Papa's naivete, shrugged her shoulders, and placed Papa's well-meant gifts on the table.

In preparation for study, I would take the morning edition of the *New York Times*, which I had bought for two cents at the candy store, and set about compulsively spreading the fresh, clean newspaper on the dining room table. But not until I had read it. This was a ritual I performed six days a week. Saturday, the Sabbath, was excluded. This accomplished, I spread my books neatly on the table, opened my notebook to a clean page, stacked my pens and pencils neatly where I could reach them easily, and started my daily studies. Now, with everything in order, I was ready to set my mind to the task of absorbing information and solving such academic problems as were assigned to me that day.

Because her daughter was approaching "sweet sixteen," Mama decided to update the apartment in preparation for the time I would start dating. Although I had not yet had a date, my mother was sure the inevitable would soon be, that I would be bringing young men home. And I thought I was duty-bound to do this. It was an obligation to my parents.

That was what they seemed to want. For my part, I thought attending to my studies took priority. In my youthful perception, education was the opposite direction from the one in which they were pushing me.

The dining room was converted into a living room. The fat-legged dining room table disappeared, as did the studio couch and buffet. Now the only flat surface for my studies was either the kitchen table or my old friend, the small psuedo-desk I had first begun to use in junior high and which now stood in the dark windowless foyer. A sofa and soft uphol-stered chairs, end tables, lamps, and a handsome breakfront now created a warm, colorful living room. This was a marked improvement over the cluttered dining room, to be sure. However, I missed the old furniture and especially the com-fortable couch on which I had been sleeping. Now I slept on a narrow folding bed in the foyer. Each morning I had to fold it up and store it in the closet. Each night I removed it from the closet and opened it out to sleep.

As the years passed, my academic work grew progressively more difficult. As I moved from grammar school to junior high to high school to college to graduate school, I moved from pseudo-desk to kitchen table to dining room table to whatever horizontal space was available to me at home. All through the years, I practiced the same tidying-up process. So it had been at the beginning, and so it was until I completed my doctorate at UCLA, and even into my postdoctoral career. I had a compulsion toward order when learning.

During the summers of our youth, Mother would take my brother and me with her to the Catskills for a two-week vaca-tion. The first time we went to the country, which is what the Catskill Mountains were called, I was three and Solly was eight. We went to Kyserike, to a farm owned by the parents of my later-to-become uncle by marriage, Morris Rappaport. The farm was a real true-to-life working farm. Hay was grown for the cows, vegetables for market, and milk was delivered to the creamery each day. To augment their income, Gershon and Chaia Rappaport had built a gray, rambling, one-story rooming house across the road from their old farmhouse. In one of the rooms of that gray house, my mother, Solly, and I slept for two weeks on several consecutive summers. A short distance behind the rooming house was another long, low building with a few gas stoves and some long tables and benches. Each guest family was entitled to one stove, one table, and two benches. Such places later became popular and were known as *koch alayns*, which means cook alone or cook for yourself. *Koch alayns* were inexpensive compared to the hotels that were rapidly beginning to spring up all over the Catskill Mountains. On weekends, Papa would come up to Kyserike before dark on Friday. Morris drove to the railroad station in his horse and buggy to pick him up. I would stand in the road excitedly waiting for them to return as the sun began to set. Papa would return to the city on Sunday night in time to open the butcher shop on Monday morning.

The very first time we went to Kyserike, I was a little girl with short, curly black hair, a deep furrowed brow, clutching desperately at my mother's skirt. The train frightened me. It had a big black engine with a tall stack that belched smoke and a high-pitched, ear-shattering whistle. To a three-year-old, it was a gigantic terrifying monster.

Mama, Solly, and I board the train and off it goes, letting off a shrill whistle every few minutes. Each time I hear this whistle it scares the "bejeebers" out of me. The train enters a tunnel. I am happy the tunnel isn't longer because my heart stops as the train goes into total darkness. Are we going to be trapped here forever? Will we ever see light again? Soon blessed sunlight floods the train and I relax. We are pulling into the station, and the stern conductor in his black uniform and billed cap is calling out "Kyserike, Kyserike." I try to descend the huge, high steps from the train to the ground, but my little legs are not long enough. The powerful conductor gathers me up in the crook of his arm with one fell swoop and sets me gently on the ground. Morris is there to meet us in a horse-drawn buggy. What a joyous ride through the open country! What a change from Brook Avenue in the dirty Bronx!

It is almost dark when we get to the old farm house. The woodstove is burning and the small low-ceilinged room is full of smoke. In front, through the windows, I can barely make out a large rambling rose bush growing over a fence, and my heart sings at the promise of so many flowers. My mother converses with Gershon and Chaia Rappaport, big-people talk. She knows them from the old country. In America, they had become owners of this farm. We eat something and cross the road to the gray house. For light, we use a kerosene lamp. Soon thousands of bugs are milling around it, smashing into it and falling dead. There are two beds in the room. I fall fast asleep on one of them, exhausted.

We returned to the farm in Kyserike each year for about four years until Mama went back to work in the butcher shop with Papa. After that, Mother said she needed rest after working hard all winter; she did not wish to cook. Also she needed a breath of fresh air. So she, Solly, and I went to a Jewish boarding house in Ellenville. In a very few years, the *koch alayns* and the plain boarding houses were being replaced by an ever-growing number of cheap hotels. And even a few fancy ones began to appear.

In the Catskill hotels, sexual banter, innuendo, and open promiscuity were the order of the day. Males chased after females, and females, unashamedly, after males. The countryside was exquisitely beautiful, pastoral and peaceful, but nobody seemed to take much notice of God's green world. Of paramount importance were eating and sex.

The main activity in these hotels was devouring unbelievable varieties of food in obscenely large amounts. With the clanging of a bell, guests came running from all corners to descend upon the dining room to feast, three times a day. The very tasty ethnic food, cholesterol and calories in total disregard, was doled out in huge amounts. One could request seconds, thirds, even fourths from the poor, overworked, underpaid waiters, usually college boys trying to save a few dollars toward next year's tuition. And one consumed as much food as one was able to stuff into one's already overloaded gut. Between meals, the kitchen was always open for yet more food on demand.

Following each of these eating orgies, one adjourned to the verandah or to the lawn and there, abandoning any thought of physical exertion, one sat in a rocking chair, rhythmically rocking back and forth, baking oneself in the sun and dozing…until it was time for the next feeding.

Billy Hodes wrote a comic Yiddish song about the goings-on in those days. In Yiddish he comically described summer vacation time in the Catskill Mountain hotels, where more and more poor working-class people thronged to escape the summer heat for a brief spell. Each verse of his song described some activity a guest might enjoy between meals if he wished. Possibly a leisurely walk through the woods (*a spatzier*), a good game of tennis, a swim in the pool, some poker or pinochle. But instead, he wrote, each activity was abandoned in favor of "*Und m' rocket sach, und m' bocket sach und me schwitzt und m' chrachet und m' grebst und m' rocket.*" This was the closing refrain of each verse. Translated, it means: "And one rocks, and one bakes oneself in the sun, and one sweats and one hacks and one belches and one rocks."

The larger hotels presented a show each night, preceded and followed by dancing to a live band in the casino. If you were a guest at one of the fancier hotels, like Grossinger's or the Concord, you were permitted to attend these shows free, but if you were a guest at a smaller hotel which did not have a social program, you needed to crash the larger hotels. My mother always chose a plain, inexpensive hotel sans social director.

Crashing always bothered me. First of all, I did not want
what I was not entitled to. Crashing made me feel like a beggar or a thief. Besides, I hated the overcrowded casinos, the
smutty stand-up comedians, and the dirty dancing. Here, one
was entertained by the later-to-become-famous stand-up
comics. I remember the likes of Jerry Lewis and Dean Martin, Buddy Hackett, and Joey Bishop, all young and just beginning to claw their way to the top with lewd, off-color rou-
tines. I found their attempts at humor repulsive; so was the
entire scene to me. Soon I refused to accompany my mother
to the country and stayed home in the sweltering summer's
heat of the city.

At school, during the academic year, I felt comfortable in
spite of the intense competition. We were all, boys and girls
alike, first-generation Americans, all being pushed by our parents to make it to the top. There, in the classroom, I fit. There
I knew that, with hard work, I could succeed. First-generation
American Jews, males especially, were neurotic high achiev-
ers. Most became doctors, lawyers, professors, and actors.
Competition was truly intense, and I, too, was caught up in
the fever. I had, at an early age, decided to make up for the
education and opportunity my parents had been denied. I
knew I was going to be a medical doctor or research scientist.
What I failed to realize was that, try as I might, the cards
were doubly stacked against me. Not only was I a girl, but I
was a Jew in a day when the plague of anti-Semitism, rampant
in Europe for generations, had been transmitted across the
ocean to infect a young America. In the early 1900s America
was openly, unashamedly both anti-Semitic and anti-feminist.

In the fall of 1933 I entered senior high school. I had my
choice of any high school in New York; I chose James Monroe
because it was the closest to home, about four miles away. For
the next two years, until the summer of 1935, I walked to and
from school in all kinds of weather. There was no swifter or

more direct route to school than by foot.

It was a long walk each day. Early mornings, during the winter months, were very cold. Many times my thighs would freeze and I lost all sensation in them. As they thawed, they ached like a sore tooth. However, one memorable, pleasant thing about the walk was passing over a bridge very close to school. Just about the time I would arrive there each morning, a long, long freight train would pass under it, clunking along. I could hear the rat-a-tat-a-tat, rat-a-tat of the cars as they rolled over the tracks. I would stand on the bridge fascinated, scanning the names on the sides of the cars. I remember Lackawanna and Western, Baltimore and Ohio, Texas Pacific, Atchison Topeka and Santa Fe, and Southern and Florida. What fascinating things were those trains carrying? Perhaps coal from Kentucky, oranges from California and Florida, lumber from Washington, or motors from Michigan. I had time to stand and dream for a few moments. One day I would have money to travel to some of those faraway places. School was just a few blocks from the bridge, and I could run if time was getting short. I would not be late. I was never late to school.

I declared myself an academic major in high school. One was either "academic," which meant you were planning to attend college, or "commercial," which meant you were planning to enter the business world. I never had any doubt about what I wished to study. My friend, Trudy Levine, lived in the same apartment house as I. She declared herself "commercial" and, upon graduation from James Monroe in 1935, got a job as a secretary earning thirty-five dollars a week, a massive amount of money in those days. I went on to Hunter College. Often Trudy would knock on my door of an evening as I sat studying at the dining room table, my books opened before me. She would say, variation on a single theme, "Hey, Ruthie, what's this all about? Come on now, what do you think you are going to earn after college? Look at me. I'll have amassed a pile of dough before you even get out of school." But I did not think of money. I knew only that I wanted an education, the best I could get.

The years 1933 to 1935 were full of turmoil. The country was in the throes of the Great Depression. Able-bodied men stood on corners selling apples for five cents apiece. Educated men were happy to have laborers' jobs; any honest work would do. My Uncle Sam's friend Gabe, a graduate engineer from Cooper-Union, was working as a laborer in a lumber yard. Soon he lost even that menial job.

In addition to the sad state of the economy, anti-Semitism took its toll. So, even if there was work, Jewish workers were the last to be hired and the first to be fired. Uncle Sam was a physician. For him it was not too bad, not as bad as for Gabe. It seemed many non-Jews wanted their doctors to be Jewish, even though they wanted little else to do with them.

The Communist and Socialist parties were very active in New York City at that time, and they started to invade the schools. The principal of James Monroe High School, Mr. Hein, was violently opposed to any kind of political activity in his school. He was a reactionary strong-armed disciplinarian who tolerated no nonsense. Nonsense to him was the entire radical movement. He wished to deny its existence. Most of the students came from homes that were poor, some seriously impoverished, but this made little difference to him. He felt no compassion for poverty. He ruled with a hard hand. He was the first American Nazi-type with whom I came into contact.

Izzie Olliker was in my class. I remember him as a curly-haired, jovial kid completely obsessed with the notion of changing the U.S. government, even if it might take bloody revolution. He sometimes frightened me; I wanted no part of his propaganda. He was either a member of the YPSL (Young People's Socialist League) or the Communist Party. I don't remember which. Many other kids in my class were also communists. But of all the radicals, Izzie was the most outspoken and vociferous. He wouldn't shut up, no matter how many times the principal warned him. Just before graduation, Izzie was expelled.

I attended a few communist and socialist rallies in those days, but never at school. I had no desire to join the radical movement. Their bully tactics and brazenness turned me off. I was all too aware of the wickedness and selfishness of big business, its unfairness and inhumanity, and of the ugliness that attended our materialistic society at that time, but I felt there must be a better, more humane way to change society. When Roosevelt appeared on the horizon in 1933, I and many other disenfranchised people began to pick up hope.

Though I found them attractive, boys terrified me. In high school, the thought of a pleasurable date might have occasionally crossed my mind, but I was never given the opportunity to have one. I was certain boys had no interest in me. Instead I poured all my energy into my studies.

I graduated from high school in June, 1935, when I was almost sixteen. In the fall of that year, I entered Hunter College.

When my brother, Solly, was in his teens, he began to date Suki. Suki Muechnik came from a poor, uncultured family. Her father was a cutter in the garment industry, commonly known as the *schmate* trade and, depending upon the vagaries of the market was in and out of work, mostly out. I remember her mother as a teary-eyed, garrulous woman who, probably through loneliness, invited any and all passersby into her apartment for tea and talk. A superb seamstress, she designed and sewed the most elegant dresses for her only daughter, Sarah.

When Sarah was fifteen, she changed her name to Suki, at which time she also changed the color of her hair from prosaic brown to exotic blond. Her pencil-slim figure was always clothed in beautiful homemade originals. She began to market her feminine wares at an early age.

One day, when Solly was home on a short break from his

dental studies at the University of Buffalo, he introduced Suki to our family as his fiancée. I was just entering college. A year or so later, when he was twenty-two, Solly married Suki. She was seventeen at the time. They eloped and were married by a justice of the peace in Buffalo.

When my parents learned of this, they ordered me to take the next Greyhound bus to Buffalo to see that their errant son, my misguided brother, be properly married by a rabbi in accordance with Jewish law. Without a Jewish marriage certificate, a *ketubah*, they were not considered wed in the eyes of God and my parents.

So off I went to Buffalo, the unwilling emissary of my family. I did not know or like Suki. But, despite his early maltreatment of me, I was devoted to my brother and, at this moment, he needed me as peacemaker.

When I arrived in Buffalo, I consulted the telephone book for a rabbi and chose one at random. After the clergyman mumbled a few incomprehensible Hebrew words, he signed a *ketubah* and then, magically, Solly and Suki were properly united.

Late Adolescence with a Few Forward Glances

Hunter College in 1935 was strictly a women's college. No men. Admission required close to an A average from high school, certainly no lower than a B.

I attended Hunter for four years, from September 1935 to June 1939, during the height of the Great Depression. Nobody, at least nobody I knew, had money. Fortunately, tuition at Hunter was absolutely free—no unit fees, no lab fees, no book fees. All the books we needed were issued to us at the beginning of the semester, to be returned at the end of class. The City of New York picked up the tab. The only financial expenses for a B.A. degree were ten dollars for a diploma and thirty dollars for a gold college ring with an amethyst stone. The latter was a luxury, not mandatory like the diploma fee. But my parents generously provided the money for both.

Hunter College courses were difficult and demanding, but one dared not complain; one was fortunate to have been admitted. As was true throughout my early school years, here there was also little room at the top. Almost all the women were bright, and competition was fierce. Grading on the curve meant a limited number of A's per class, and it was difficult to get one.

The original Hunter College building was on 68th Street in Manhattan, but new buildings had been built in the Bronx following a major fire in the original building. The first two years of my college life were spent in the new Bronx buildings. The grounds were still not landscaped and, when it rained, we had to wade through deep mud to get from one building to another. Although the labs were neat and adequately furnished, the school did not possess the warm patina of an aged academic institution like Columbia, which I later attended.

For the second two years before graduation, all science majors were transferred to a skyscraper in downtown Manhattan. Several floors had been converted to classrooms and laboratories. The rest of the building was for the use of businesses and corporations not associated with Hunter. Crowded elevators transported students as well as businesspeople from one floor to another. Attending classes amidst the commercial bustle of a Manhattan skyscraper was no way to enjoy college life.

Like all New York public schools I had attended, Hunter was impersonal. Most professors took little more than a casual interest in their students. This was sad because I, especially, needed guidance. I was very young, and there was nobody at home to counsel me. I yearned to be a pre-med student. My parents strictly forbade it on the advice of my conservative, anti-feminist, university-trained Uncle Joe, who, they felt, knew all the answers to American academic questions.

"We will not pay for sending you to medical school. No man in his right mind will want to marry a woman doctor! Solly goes to medical school, not you," my mother chided. "Teaching is the best profession for women, now that teachers are permitted to marry. Men like teachers for wives. Be a teacher." It did not matter whether being a schoolteacher was of interest to me or not.

In those days there were no scholarships available for women medical students. Without one, there was no possible way for me to attend, so I had no alternative but to take a natural science major with a minor in education (pedagogy), on my way to becoming a high school science teacher. I took all the coursework necessary for such a major, a smorgasbord of the sciences—human physiology, botany, chemistry, anthropology, physics, bacteriology, comparative anatomy, embryology, paleontology, and geology. The one course that truly intrigued me was botany. Botany was a strange choice for a girl from the Bronx, where nothing grew except in the orderly Bronx Botanical Gardens, in the few parks, or randomly between the cracks in the cement city streets.

Why did I have such an inexplicable, avid interest in plants? I can't say with certainty except that from the first moment I can remember, I passionately loved flowers and all green things that grew and blossomed. Plants filled my world with beauty. As a child I grew all sorts of them in pots and jars on our fire escape, despite my mother's constant railing. "There is a law against growing plants on the fire escape. They will throw you in jail if you don't stop doing this." But how could I live without plants? In spite of my family's prohibition against my becoming a medical doctor, I could envision myself obtaining a Ph.D. in botany without requiring their financial approval or support. So, if they would not permit me to be an M.D., I would become a Ph.D. on my own and then teach and do research in a university. That would suit me. I was convinced that my life's pursuit was academic research in some phase of botany, bacteriology, or microbiology. I did not want to teach high school; I slept through all my pedagogy courses.

The semester of general botany with Professor Cross convinced me that I was right in wishing to pursue some phase of plant science. My instructor was totally dispassionate. She showed no special interest in me, nor did she display any excitement for her chosen field of expertise. She was in her late forties and married. I knew this because she wore a marriage ring. She never spoke of personal matters. We called her by her title, Professor Cross. Her first name was Olive, an appropriate name for a botanist. Her lectures were brimful of interesting material, which I devoured. The class required a great deal of memorization, but, despite this, the subject fascinated me, not because Professor Cross made it interesting with ar-

dor or enthusiasm, but because her material was so well organized. I resonated to the ordinate, logical way in which she
presented her lectures. And it explained to me how my beloved plants grew. Later, when I was already an ordained
Ph.D. botanist, I realized that much of her lecture material
was based on a nineteenth-century text by Ganong. This was a
fascinating book, uncomplicated by the then-modern-day
chemistry, genetics, or technology. It read almost like a
storybook. And so did her course appear to me. It was science, but fascinating, much like a story.

My next advanced course in botany was mycology, the
study of fungi. This course was dull because the professor
made it so. A sad-faced little woman, Dr. Granick always
seemed on the verge of tears. I put excitement into the course
myself by studying the texts to learn more than her lectures
conveyed. When I became adept at using the microscope, I
was captivated by the diversity and perfection of the fungi,
beauty that could be detected only when using the high power
of a fine microscope. I was determined to be a botanist with a
specialty in mycology.

On the other hand, I really disliked zoology, especially
comparative anatomy and embryology. While human physiology interested me, I probably would not have made a good
medical doctor, despite my desire to be one. I could not mus-
ter enough interest in bones, nerves, joints, and muscles to
master their tedious origins, insertions, and actions. And I
later learned that women M.D.s did not fare much better
than women Ph.D. scientists in my day. I chose the science I
instinctively loved and could financially pursue without support from my parents.

In high school, in the statewide English Regents exam, I
had scored above 90 percent. If I had any notion of my superiority in English, it was quickly dashed when I encountered
my first college English instructor.

Each week, in class, we were given a topic of her choice.
In forty-five minutes we were to produce an original composi-

tion on that topic. There was no time to compose carefully. No time to correct. The composition had to be written and presented just as it came, hot off the griddle.

My first paper was graded A/D, A for content, D for composition. The comment at the top of the page read: "Use shorter words, words you truly understand!" By the end of the term, I received a final grade of B. This instructor's assessment of my ability as a writer convinced me that I really was not as good an English student as I had thought.

The next semester I took a survey course in poetry which concerned itself with the early English poets. We had just finished reading "An Elegy Written in a Country Churchyard" by Sir Thomas Gray, a poem which dates to about 1740.

The curfew tolls the knell of parting day,
The lowing herd winds slowly o'er the lea,
The plowman homeward plows his weary way,
And leaves the world to darkness and to me.

Now fades the glimmering landscape on the sight
And all the air a solemn stillness holds,
Save where the beetle wheels his droning flight,
And drowsy tinkling lulls the distant folds.

I loved poetry, especially this poem. I could see a peaceful, pastoral English countryside at sundown, all life slowing down. The authoritarian Dr. Babette Deutsch, my instructor, dismissed Thomas Gray's piece as "ordinary." "Gray," she said, "did nothing more than copy the other poets of the period. He made no original contribution."

Her sharp judgment disturbed me. It was not usual for me to expound in class. I disliked calling attention to myself. But her criticism stirred me to rebuttal. I raised my hand, "Yes?" she said. Passionately, with heart racing, frightened to contradict a professor, I said, "I do not feel there is anything in the world written or created that is totally original. I think we build on what has gone before and add our individual interpretation to that which already is. I think Gray's poem is beautiful." I sat down. The class and the instructor heard me without comment, and we moved on to other things. But in later years, when I was doing original research, I was scrupulous in ferreting out any and all investigations which had preceded mine. I built on what had gone before.

When I had finished my required four semesters of English, Dr. Blanche Colton Williams, chairperson of the English department, invited me to come in to see her. "In light of your performance in your English classes, I would like to invite you to become an English major," she said without enthusiasm.

With whom could I discuss this matter? Perhaps my parents cared, but they had no advice to give. Besides, my mother had already made the decision that I was to be a high school teacher. She didn't care if it were English or biology or home economics, so I said, "No, thanks. I'll stay with science. I want to be a research scientist." She gave me no argument.

I might have given her words more consideration had she explained to me that were I to pursue a career in English, I might have had some chance at a university position. Better a professorship in English than no university career at all! Had only somebody at Hunter taken time to know me, to hear my wishes, to explain that women's time in the sciences had not yet come, that I was indeed an excellent English student with a possible academic future. Robert Frost's poem, so often quoted, comes to mind. Of the two roads which diverged in a yellow wood, that day I chose the one less travelled. I would be a scientist.

Graduation from Hunter in June 1939 was uneventful. I felt empty and desolate. I did not feel educated, nor had I been academically recognized in any way. There was still so much to learn. I knew it would be a long, hard struggle to the doctorate in science, but I was ready to start, determined to attain it, to gain recognition as a scholar. I knew I could do it.

•

Graduation over, I had the summer free until fall, when I would attend Columbia University. The newspapers were full of the maniacal ravings of Adolph Hitler. He swore to annihilate all Jews, the vermin of the world. America, the country in which I had been born and to which I had sworn allegiance every morning as a schoolchild, did not love Jews either. That was apparent by the vacillation of President Roosevelt as well as by the attitude of a rigid State Department toward Jewish refugees fleeing Germany. Those people, desperately seeking asylum in America, had no choice but to return to their deaths in their native land. At Columbia, rumor had it that Jewish students were accepted on a six percent quota basis.

The summer of 1939 I spent as a nature-study counselor at Camp Silverwood. To that beautiful, prestigious camp, built in a magnificent forest of evergreens, came the spoiled offspring of affluent parents. The campers had all the material things I had been denied in my growing up, and I resented them. But, like it or not, it was better for me to spend the summer in wooded Pittsfield, Massachusetts, than in New York City with its sweltering heat and humidity. Better to be amongst the tall trees in the Berkshires than in the concrete jungle of New York. Besides, I would be earning the monumental sum of fifty dollars for six weeks' work. A bunk bed and board came along with it. Fifty dollars would help pay for some of my texts at Columbia in the fall.

On one of my nights off, I heard that the Boston Symphony was playing at Tanglewood under the baton of Serge Kousevitzky. It was August, and I and another female counselor decided to hitchhike the twenty miles from camp to Tanglewood. By the time we arrived, night had begun to fall. The evening was mild, and the stars shone clear and bright in the sky. The audience was receptive and excited as if something wonderful were about to happen. And indeed it did! The orchestra played magnificently, and then came the unannounced surprise! Kousevitzky handed the baton to a handsome young man, introducing to the public for the first time his most talented student, Leonard Bernstein. Bernstein's first concert was truly magical. My spirits soared. Bernstein and I, I learned later, shared a birthday, August 11, 1919.

When the music was over, the difficult task of returning to camp faced us. We had given no thought to our return in the night. There was no public transportation available. Getting there during daylight was no big chore, but now it was deep night.

We set off down the dark country road, stopping now and then to thumb a ride. We knew hitchhiking might be dangerous, but we had no alternative. We had to get back before sunrise.

Soon a car pulled over. We got in, my friend in front with the driver, and I in the rumble seat with another young man. It was dark, very dark, and the country roads were totally deserted. I tried to make conversation, but talk went over with a dull thud. The more I talked, the harder he tried to engage me in sex. I resisted, but to no avail. He pressed harder until I began to scream. I thought surely he would kill me if I did not acquiesce. He fought. I fought back. Maybe my screams frightened the driver, because he suddenly stepped on the brakes and the car screeched to a halt on the unpaved country road, raising a cloud of dust. My friend and I were both peremptorily dumped into the darkness. It was scary in the night, two girls alone, but not as terrifying as being in the car with the men. We walked the rest of the way back to camp, a long, hard hike, arriving in the early morning hours.

This experience further galvanized my fear of men. Why was a woman's "no" ignored? Was male sexuality so unfeeling, so brutal? Were all men that egocentric, that single-minded?

Each of the confusing sexual encounters I had experienced during my early life increased my suspicion of men. To me, the male sex drive seemed to be based on irrational passion verging on violence rather than on love and gentleness.

With so much fear, I did not know how to cope with my feminine feelings. "I cannot solve this problem. Safer to withdraw," I thought in denial. I made a firm commitment to stay with my studies.

Before applying for admission to Columbia, I had received two offers from graduate schools, one a scholarship in biology to Boston University, and another a laboratory assistantship in botany at the University of Arizona in Tucson. My mother quickly quashed both options. Boston University's administration insisted that at my age, nineteen going on twenty, I must live in their dormitories. If I were to do this, I would deplete the entire sum the scholarship offered. I explained that I could live with my relatives in Malden, only eight miles away, and commute into Boston each day. Their rules were fixed and immutable: under twenty-one, live in the dorms! My parents were unable or unwilling to make up the difference in the money I would need for tuition. So much for Boston.

As for the University of Arizona, my mother insisted that Arizona was too far from home. Furthermore, she said seriously, there were probably only Indians living that far west, certainly no Jews. For a woman who had at eighteen courageously crossed the Atlantic to a strange, totally unknown land, why was she so protective—or controlling—of me?

By then I had no more time to apply for other funding. But I had saved enough money to pay my tuition to Columbia, enough for a master's degree. Through the years, birthday money and Chanukah *gelt* had been frugally, carefully stashed away in the Dollar Savings Bank, earning interest. And I could easily afford eleven dollars per graduate unit. I could live at home, sleep on a folding cot, and use my small pseudo-desk in the dark foyer as study space. My parents offered me bed and board without cost. I had no choice. Columbia it was.

From the time I was sixteen, my mother had been constantly harping that I go out with boys, wear more make-up, discard my boring eyeglasses, and pretend to be stupid when on a date. Her advice irritated me. If I were ever to snare a

man, and to her way of thinking I was obliged to, I must follow her duplicitous rules.

One day, out of respect for her wishes rather than my
own, I left my lab at Columbia earlier than usual to attend a
Jewish Graduate Student Society meeting on campus. I
walked from the lab in Schermerhorn to the law building a
short distance away. There, in one of the classrooms, a number of graduate students had gathered. One young man asked
if he might walk back to my lab with me following the meeting. He was a law student, working for a juris doctor degree.
He was a pleasant, good-looking, respectable young man. I
wondered what attracted him to me. I felt like a laboratory
mouse who had just been liberated from its cage. I didn't
know quite how to act.

After that initial meeting, we saw each other frequently
for several months. He lived in Brooklyn. I should have understood that he was indeed interested in me if he was willing
to make the long, arduous subway journey from Brooklyn to
the Bronx to pick me up, take me to a show in Manhattan,
bring me back to the Bronx, and then go home to Brooklyn.
These occasions must have brought him home in the wee
hours of the morning.

But I kept searching for his motive. Why was he putting
so much effort into seeing me? Why didn't he explain, clearly
and simply, what I meant to him? In retrospect, I understand
that he would have been unable to reach me even if he had
hired an orchestra to play paeans to my attributes. At twenty,
I was already seriously withdrawn sexually. While I truly
wanted love, I did not know how to accept it. Neither did I
know how to give it.

All through my young years Papa had spoken fervently
and openly against sex. "Those girls," he would say looking out
the window of our apartment, "those, there, you see them?
Those standing on the corner under the lamppost with the
boys? Those girls are *kurves*, prostitutes. See the way they flirt
with the boys? See how they laugh? Soon they will be in deep

trouble." With this admonition ringing in my head, how could I be intimate with a man and not be a *kurve*? I was programmed early against sex, programmed to see it as ugly and lewd—except in a respectable marriage.

Time and again, Joe made the long journey from Brooklyn to the Bronx. The very last night I saw him, we attended a concert at the Lewisohn Stadium at City College. As we walked from the subway to the stadium, he proposed marriage. Quietly, with no fanfare, no preamble, he said: "Ruthie, let's get married."

I was taken completely off guard. What to say? It took me a few moments before I could bring myself to respond.

"No, Joe," I said, "I'm not interested in marriage. I'm interested in test tubes, Petri dishes, microorganisms. I'm not interested in washing pots and pans in a kitchen. Please don't ask me to explain, but I feel a career in science is more important than one in domesticity."

I was twenty at the time and did not know what sexual love meant. All my love had been poured into my studies. Two weeks later Joe married another woman. I was stunned by the news. Both my motives and judgment were suspect. Did I truly want a career exclusively? Did I secretly, deep in my heart, want marriage? Could it be that I wanted both? I only knew that sex outside of marriage was unthinkable. Academia seemed to be a safe haven.

Joe was not the only man I turned away. I did it several times, not with a clear wish to hurt, but out of confusion. By twenty, I had already been thoroughly brainwashed against sex. Between Papa's intolerance of "flirting" and Mama's devious, "get a man," I did not know which way to go. Unfortunately, my parents did not encourage me in my wish for a career in science. To them marriage was the only acceptable path for a woman. But I was not yet ready to accept marriage as a substitute for an academic career.

My Uncle Morris was the first real love of my young life. I had known him from the time I was three, when my Mother took me on my first vacation to his parents' farm in Kyserike. At that time he was still a medical student. In the summer, away from the university, he worked on the farm, milking cows, taking the milk to the creamery at the end of the day, chucking hay, doing whatever farm chores needed doing. I was a curly-haired little girl with big brown eyes. I was called *"de schwartze,"* the black one, because unlike anybody else in my family, I was swarthy.

As a small child on the farm, I shadowed Morris. Wherever he turned, I was there. Often in the early evening he would lift me into the horsedrawn two-seater buggy to sit beside him. With milk cans rattling in the back, we would drive down the tree-lined country road to the creamery. He called me Rutchicle, a name I have treasured all my life, a name nobody else has ever used. It was a special bond between us. He always wore a short white doctor's coat while doing farm chores, and I thought he was wonderful. Years later, when I was thirteen, he married Aunt Sarah, my mother's youngest sister.

After the wedding the bride and groom moved to Massachusetts and there made their home. It was in Malden that Morris started a medical practice. For years, until I graduated from Columbia and finally left New York City for good, I would visit my Aunt Sarah and Uncle Morris each Christmas vacation and for several days each summer. Whenever I visited Malden, Morris would invite me to drive with him to the hospital, where he made his daily rounds. I would sit in the car waiting for him, dreaming I might also be a doctor one day.

An aside: One day, on our way home from the hospital, Uncle Morris and I stopped at a restaurant in Malden Square, a small collection of shops, precursor to the larger malls that followed in later years.

Morris, opening his menu, said: "Order anything you like, but, Rutchicle, I'd advise a bacon, lettuce, and tomato sandwich. It's great."

I was sixteen at the time and had never before eaten food that was not kosher. Bacon, from a pig, was *traif*, forbidden. A pig did not have cloven hooves, nor a four-chambered stomach, nor did it chew its cud. It was unacceptable food for a Jew.

"Eat it, eat it, you'll like it," he urged, noting my hesitation. "Time you grew up." My dearest Uncle Morris led me on my first steps away from the cloistered kosher life of the New York ghetto.

Early Adulthood—
Columbia University _____

I enjoyed graduate school at Columbia. If there was anti-Semitism practice there, I was not aware of it. But having come from Hunter, where the student population was almost totally Jewish, I was aware that I was the only full-time Jewish student in the botany department. But then, I thought, what right-thinking New York Jew, who couldn't tell a rose from a daisy, wanted to study botany? It was an impractical field that led only to a few research jobs, poor paying at that. So I was the only New York Jew that year to be a full-time graduate student in botany at Columbia.

There were many part-time students in the department, most of them employed teachers taking one course a semester to fulfill Board of Education requirements. Some were working piecemeal toward graduate degrees. The regular cadre of full-time students consisted of only four: Ann Hansen, Victor Larsen, Libro Ajello, and me.

Victor was teaching at Adelphi College in the evenings. Libro went on to become a renowned mycologist with the Centers for Disease Control and Prevention in Atlanta. Unlike me, he did not enter the armed forces, but continued his studies during the war. Ann Hansen died before graduating.

While I loved my work, the year spent at Columbia was not a leisurely one. The academic work was quite advanced for a student as inexperienced as I. Since Hunter had no graduate program, I had not had training in research methods. Course material there was usually carefully structured by the professors and required no original thinking on the student's part, merely memorization and regurgitation. It was obvious that the professors at Hunter were not research oriented.

Graduate school was quite different. From the carefully delineated undergraduate program to which I was accustomed, I moved to the *laissez-faire* system of Columbia's graduate school. I was free to choose my coursework, plan my study program, and proceed at my own pace. I matriculated for three full-year courses: mycology, plant physiology, and cytology. My major professor was Dr. John Karling. He taught both mycology and cytology. He was also in charge of my thesis research. His lab assistant was a quiet, unobtrusive young man, a Ph.D. candidate, Arthur Hillegas.

Dr. Karling assigned me a research topic for my master's thesis. He had collected specimens of Common Milkweed (*Asclepias syriaca*) from fields in the palisades on the New Jersey side of the Hudson River. This species, an insignificant weed, was being threatened with extinction. He was sure it was due to a fungus that was attacking the root systems of the plants. He handed me a bag of moribund plants and, without further elaboration, said, "Find the pathogen."

"How do you do this?" I asked.

"That's for you to discover," he answered. "Ask Mr. Hillegas for help. Good day." With that he turned back to his microscope. I was dismissed.

What does one do with this sack of sick stuff? Wash it? Plant it? I did not have a clue as to how to isolate a pathogen from diseased plant tissue. When I found Hillegas, he was as cryptic and evasive as his professor.

I went to the library to search for information. On my own, without guidance, it took me weeks to learn how to isolate a pathogen from diseased plant tissue. By then, time had passed and the plants which I had placed in a moist chamber were completely overgrown with mold. What to do now? Was all this fuzzy stuff the killer? Too late I discovered that I should have immediately sterilized the exterior surfaces of the roots before placing them in a moist chamber; there were many saprophytes on the root surfaces which I had failed to eliminate. Also I should have excised the interior root tissue and cultured only that. This would have yielded only the pathogen. Now it was too late; the roots were completely overgrown with the intertwining mycelia of many different fungi, probably including the mycelia of the culprit pathogen. In my ignorance of proper isolation techniques, I ended up not with the single pathogenic fungus I was seeking, but rather with eight assorted ones, all but one of which were known saprophytes. I was sure I had hopelessly flubbed it.

When I nervously, desperately, consulted Dr. Karling to request fresh plant material, he said, "Run with it. I have no more tissue. Identify the pathogen from what you have." But which of the eight had killed the milkweed?

Since I had isolated a variety of organisms, I felt it necessary to describe each one. Back to the library and the complicated keys with which I was to identify my specimens. I was not yet conversant with all the Latin and scientific jargon used in the keys. There were lots of new technical words, lots to unravel, lots to learn, lots to study under the microscope. Research is hard digging, I thought. Finally, after months of work, I identified eight fungi. One of the eight was a new form, as yet undescribed in the literature. I described it. It was a *Chaetomium* species. A feather in my cap, but not the answer to my problem. Which one was the killer?

Of all the fungi I had isolated, only one was suspect, a member of the pathogenic genus *Fusarium*. Hard as I tried, I could not key it beyond genus to species. All the other fungi I had isolated were saprophhytes, that is, fungi known to live in the air, in the soil, or on the surface of healthy tissue, never killer organisms. *Fusarium* it must be! But if I were to be absolutely certain of this, I reasoned, I would have to grow healthy *Asclepias* plants from seed, inoculate them with each of the fungi I had isolated, and wait to see which plants died.

I approached Dr. Karling to request *Asclepias* seed. I could foresee months and months of hard work ahead, planting and inoculating. But by this time, happily, Dr. Karling was satisfied that my work was enough to support a master's thesis. Thank God!

Producing a thesis had taught me the techniques of mycological research. I had become familiar with the literature and the Latin keys well enough to identify all the fungi I had isolated. At no point in my work had I received much help from either Dr. Karling or his teaching assistant. This *laissez-faire* method of teaching was new to me and very difficult for an unsophisticated freshman graduate student. However, I am grateful to Dr. Karling for his brand of "non-teaching." Certainly, on my own, minimally guided, I had learned a great deal.

My courses were very intensive, especially the laboratory parts. In plant cytology, I often spent from early morning until late at night waiting for onion root-tip cells to divide. I do not know why mitosis occurs only during the night; however, because of this I had to be present in the lab late at night and into the wee hours of the morning, cutting, sectioning, and fixing root-tips in alcohol. My goal was to find representative examples of the various stages of chromosome division—interphase, prophase, anaphase, telophase, and, finally, cell division. Using a *camera lucida*, I had to draw chromosomal activity as it progressed through the night. Today this work might be more easily done using photomicroscopy. But in 1940 *camera lucida* drawings were *the* way, a very time-consuming process. My labors often took me until one or two in the morning. Then there was the subway ride home. The walk from the subway to my home so late at night, through the unlighted park, was scary and dangerous. And then, after a few hours of sleep, back to Columbia by 8:00 A.M.

In addition to three lectures per week in each of my courses, there were exams to take and laboratory notebooks to hand in from time to time. Then there was my own research. I was one busy lady! I figured that, with diligence, I could get all of this done in one academic year, and I almost did... almost.

One night, toward suppertime, I became involved in sectioning onion root-tips and could not tear myself away long enough to get something to eat. Against such emergencies I kept a kosher salami in my microscope cabinet, unrefrigerated of course. This night I used my scalpel to cut off a slab, and while intently searching through the microscope for cellular activity, I nibbled away at the salami. It tasted okay, but I was too absorbed in my work to consider taste. As the night wore on, I began to feel sick. Despite this, I continued on with my work. By the time I stumbled home late that night, I was very ill, running a temperature, and had terrible cramping pain cutting across my abdomen.

Very early in the morning, unable to tolerate the pain any longer, I called my Uncle Sam. He came at once. I had appendicitis, he said, and would have to go to the hospital.

"Sorry," I said, "impossible. The academic year is winding down and I am in the midst of final exams. Also, I need to finish my thesis, or my degree will be held up."

He didn't answer, but went to the phone and made a call. Very soon another doctor appeared. He palpated my abdomen. I doubled up in pain.

"You'll have to come with me," he said. "This is an emergency. I'll need to take your appendix out immediately."

Again I remonstrated. Then he told me about a classmate of his who had been in the same predicament as I. He also had refused to yield to emergency surgery because it was final exam time.

"But," the surgeon said, "he never became a doctor. He died of peritonitis."

With that, I accepted his offer of an automobile ride to French Hospital, where surgery proceeded immediately.

My Uncle Sam was present in the operating room, as

were the surgeon and several young residents. I had been given a spinal and was quite alert. The surgery proceeded. I had no sensation from the waist down. In fact, I was feeling pretty good. And then I became aware of the conversation between the doctors. "Look at this," I heard someone say with some excitement. "See how small her ovaries are. Hmm...very interesting." At that point I piped up from under the sheets, where everybody thought I was dozing. "Yes," I said, "that's atrophy through disuse, part of the Lamarckian theory of evolution, you know."

I remember laughter. I remember no more. I must have been given another shot to keep me quiet.

I had learned my biology well and remembered the Lamarckian theory of evolution, which dealt with the inheritance of acquired characteristics. In 1801, J.B. Lamarck proclaimed that organs in animals became stronger or weaker, became more or less important, through use or disuse. These changes, he felt, were transmitted from parent to progeny. While most scientists today, like those of his day, do not hold with Lamarck's theory, the concept of "atrophy through disuse" interested me and, at that precise moment, seemed appropriate to my situation—well, at least to my tranquilized mind.

An aside: The cockroaches at Columbia University were the largest and most impressive I have ever seen, even larger than those I later encountered when I was in the Navy at the Norfolk Navy Yard. Columbia, or King's College as it was originally called, was founded long before the American Revolution. I am certain the cockroaches of 1939 were direct descendants of that aristocratic lineage. If a person were to enter a laboratory late at night and suddenly switch on the lights, one would see these mighty creatures scurrying for cover. They were fully two inches long and almost as wide. I blame them for my ill-timed appendicitis attack. Perhaps they had gotten to my salami before me that fateful night.

•

One day in 1939 there was a great stir in Schermerhorn. The building was abuzz. People were standing about the corridors in small groups talking excitedly. Franz Boas had escaped from Germany and was coming to Columbia's biology department as a guest professor! Dr. Boas was one of the world's most renowned anthropologists and a Jew. My reactions were several: great pride in a fellow Jew of such eminence; overwhelming terror concerning his expulsion from the land of his birth; and gripping fear that such an atrocity might occur to me and my fellow Jews in our native America. I disappeared into my lab, busied myself with my work, and did not wait to greet him.

Before entering the hospital for my appendectomy I had turned in my plant physiology notebook for grading. It was the end of the academic year. When my notebook was returned, Dave Taylor, Dr. Trelease's lab assistant, had written across the top of it: "A+. This notebook is good, the best! Were you drunk or asleep when you typed it?" And my typing has not improved over the years.

I had taken my final plant physiology and cytology exams before my surgery. Only mycology remained. I requested a make-up exam. Dr. Karling set the time for one week after my return from the hospital. I spent that week studying at my little pseudo-desk in the dark foyer. Following the surgery, my back ached like a sore tooth, but I felt compelled to finish studying despite it. My thesis had yet to be completed. Also, my bench in plant physiology needed to be cleaned up and vacated.

I took a cab to Columbia, an extravagance in which I had never before indulged. But this was an emergency. In an empty classroom, all alone, I took my exam. Then I went upstairs to the plant physiology lab and slowly, laboriously, cleaned up my bench. Everything was now complete except for my thesis. Some work still needed to be done; spore measurements and *camera lucida* drawings remained to be finished. For the next few weeks, I pressed on with my work. It was 1940. The country was still in a severe economic depression. I was worried about how I would earn a wage after graduation. I was certain my parents would not evict me, but I knew it was a large financial burden for them to continue to feed, house, and clothe me. I was twenty years old, and it was time to make a living. In my last semester at Columbia, I had filled out numerous applications for federal, state, and private employment, applying for any job, anywhere. I may have contacted half the states in the union. Nobody showed any interest in me.

In desperation, I volunteered my services in the plant pathology research labs of the Bronx Botanical Gardens. Secretly I hoped this might lead to a paying job. In addition, I wished to experience first hand how a botanist applies his or her research toward solving a practical problem. When I had asked Dr. Karling how and with what chemicals one sprayed an ailing tree, he answered: "Any moron can spray a tree." His elitist answer did not satisfy me.

At the Bronx Botanical Gardens I worked with Dr. B.O. Dodge for a few hours each week. Time moved on, but no money was forthcoming. The economy had not yet turned around. Although I was unpaid, it was a privilege to work with so eminent a scientist as Dr. Dodge and, indeed, from him I learned a great deal about the practical aspects of plant pathology. But I could not stay on without a salary.

Fortunately, in late July I received a telegram from Washington, D.C., offering me a position as a statistical clerk at the Bureau of the Census, Department of Commerce, Washington, D.C. The salary was $1,440 per year, five and one half days per week. With no other job on the horizon, I leaped at the opportunity, glad to have any honest paying work, any straw to grasp.

•

When I arrived in Washington, I discovered that many

other Hunter graduates had received a telegram identical to mine. It seemed Washington wanted the entire Hunter class of '39. Soon I discovered why.

Federal census was taken in 1940. Throughout the United States, census takers were knocking on doors, in cities, on farms. By hand, they were recording population statistics in large, unwieldy books. "Who lives in this house? What is the marital status of each occupant? How many members are there in this family? Is anyone here self-employed? What occupations and industries are the people living in this home involved in?" On and on they questioned. My job, and that of hundreds of other young college-trained people, was to code the occupations and industries of the American population. Computers were not yet available for this task; without them the work was mind-boggling.

Through all my years in New York, I had yearned to live in a rural area, away from a big city. In 1940 the center of Washington, D.C., was already big and growing. However, the outskirts were still rural. So I moved into a house on Delafield Street N.W., which, in those days, was a distance out in the third alphabet, where the city was still relatively undeveloped.

I rented a room in the house of two sisters, both spinster teachers, both dour and uncommunicative. The house was as sterile as their personalities. My second-floor bedroom was spartan, but this did not distress me, since I spent very little time there. I had practically no discourse with the ladies at any time.

We worked a half-day on Saturday. The other half-day afforded me some pleasurable relaxation. I wandered around Washington sightseeing; there was much of interest to see. But, more often, driven by my desire to complete my thesis, I went to the Department of Agriculture lab to work.

When I had received the telegram from Washington in August 1940, I approached Dr. Karling regarding my thesis; minor details still remained to be completed. He suggested I pack my Petri dishes and test tubes and take them along to

Washington. A friend of his, Dr. Charles Thom, a world-renowned mycologist, was in charge of the plant pathology laboratories of the United States Department of Agriculture. Dr. Karling wrote a letter for me to deliver to Dr. Thom asking if it was possible to make room for me in one of the USDA labs so that I could finish my research.

Dr. Thom generously offered me a small lab in his department and issued me a key. I worked there whenever I found free time, depending on my job schedule. Often I found myself working in this huge locked building all alone nights and weekends.

At the end of nine months in Washington, in addition to my full-time job, I had completed my research. I am most grateful to Dr. Thom for permitting me the use of the labs and library of the USDA. Because of his generosity, I was able to complete the identification of all the fungal forms I had isolated. And I also finished most of the writing. Now I needed to go home, organize my material, have the thesis typed by somebody more proficient than me, and present it to Dr. Karling for approval.

I notified my landladies that I would be returning home to New York in a few weeks. Leisurely leafing through the *Washington Post* one day, looking for nothing in particular, I inadvertently spied an ad: "Room to rent in a nice Christian home; 409 Delafield Place N.W. Only Christians need apply." That was *my* address!

I was humiliated and furious. They had obviously not recognized me as a Jew, or they would not have rented to me. On a much more serious global note, wasn't this what was happening to Jews in Germany? Pious, church-going German Christians, like these two pious women in Washington, wore false faces. What had happened to the Judeo-Christian ethic: "Love thy neighbor as thyself?" Perhaps my parents were right…Jews belonged with Jews. I was quite ready to leave Washington.

•

Back home, I returned to Columbia. My thesis was entitled, "Some Fungi Isolated from the Decaying Root of *Asclepias syriaca*." Dr. Karling approved it. I then presented it to Dr. Trelease, head of the botany department and my plant physiology professor, for his approval. He invited me to sit as he turned the pages and studied the accompanying drawings. After a few minutes, he looked up sternly and, quite off-point, said, "How many varieties of gladiolus are growing on this campus?"

I was taken aback by the unexpected question. This had absolutely nothing to do with my thesis! Frankly, I had never been aware of a single gladiolus or anything else growing on campus. When I came into the light of day from the subway tunnel each day, I walked the one block to the university, up the huge flight of outdoor stairs, past the law library building, on to Schermerhorn, up the elevator to the third floor into my lab, and that was it. From then on, until I left at night for home, I never looked to the right or left, intent upon getting to my microscope and my day's work.

Were there plants growing on campus? I remembered only steps, the red brick walls of Schermerhorn, the tall columns and concrete walls of the law library. I panicked!

"Dr. Trelease," I said, "I have no knowledge of *any* gladiolus growing on campus."

"Ruth," he said, "we cannot award a master's degree in botany from Columbia University to any of our students who cannot name at least twenty varieties of gladiolus growing on campus." And then seeing my dismay and confusion, he laughed at his joke and signed my page. "Good work," he said. My thesis was accepted.

In June, 1941, I attended my graduation from Columbia. There was a virtual sea of academically garbed graduates of all sorts, B.A.s, M.A.s, Ph.D.s, M.D.s, D.D.S.s, L.L.D.s...everybody graduating at once. I abhor hordes, so being one of so many afforded me no pleasure. Besides, I was yearning for more education. I felt almost as unfinished and unrecognized as I had when I received my B.A. from Hunter. When I receive my Ph.D., I thought, I will feel fulfilled. I will then know everything there is to know in my field. It was naive thinking, but it served to spur me on.

If all had gone well with the world, I might have finished my doctorate at Columbia in one more year, two at the most. But all was not right with the world. I was young, not yet twenty-one. In addition, in order to continue my education I would need financial help from my parents. Did I dare ask for more when they had already given so much beyond what they could afford?

Hitler was rapidly swallowing Europe up piece by piece. A frightened, wavering world was not objecting, at least not vehemently. England's Chamberlain had just signed a *friendship* pact with Hitler. As an American Jew, I knew anti-Semitism to be quite prevalent, even popular, in the United States. It seemed entirely plausible to me that Hitler might cross the Atlantic. Then what would be my fate and that of my people? While I felt sure the United States would put up a struggle should Hitler invade us, I was not certain how much enthusiasm Americans might put into the fight. Did the United States feel Jews were worth defending? Yet certainly, I tried to reassure myself, the Jewish issue was not the sole determinant of whether the United States went to war against Germany. I was sure there were other pressing issues of which I was not aware. I felt fear both as an American and, especially, as a Jew.

One day in 1941, while still mopping up at Columbia, I had a dream which determined my future. I was alone at the top of a tall tower, from which I had a three-hundred-sixty-degree view in all directions. Fires burned everywhere as far as my eyes could see, even to the foot of the tower. How could I escape? The tower would certainly be consumed if the flames were not quickly extinguished. Would I perish? How could I avoid the holocaust?

When I awoke, my heart pounding, I knew with certainty

that I could not continue studying while the world burned. Furthermore, on a very practical level, Columbia's campus had been blacked out. At night dark shades were drawn at all the windows. Street lights were extinguished. All was black. When I tried to walk the several blocks from the subway to my lab or from my lab to the greenhouse, I could not see the way. And it was dangerous to be alone on the streets. Although obtaining the Ph.D. was very close to my heart, I knew it would have to wait until the world settled down, if it ever did.

On one of my frequent visits to my relatives in Malden following the completion of my master's degree, I attempted to find war-related work. In Boston I went into the office of the U.S. Army Corps of Engineers on Milk Street. Only a few months had elapsed since I left Washington, and I thought I might be able to effect a transfer from my Washington job to one in Boston. As it turned out, I could. I wished to contribute whatever I could to the war effort. Where better than the War Department?

I was interviewed by a young lieutenant named Sargent. We had a long, amiable chat. I asked him if perchance he were related to the artist. Yes, he was. And that made for friendly conversation. We laughed together heartily when I made a pun at his expense. I said: "You are the first lieutenant I've ever met who is also a sergeant." Finally, he asked the pertinent question: "Can you type?"

"Oh, yes," I lied through my teeth, recalling the comment Dave Taylor had written at the top of my plant physiology lab notebook: "Were you drunk or asleep when you typed this?"

Fortunately, in the flush of our conversation, Lt. Sargent forgot to have me prove my typing skills. If he had, I would have failed miserably. "Report to work in three weeks," he said as we shook hands.

I had three weeks to improve my hunt-and-peck typing. The little, loyal Royal portable, which my parents had purchased for me as a graduation present, had not been used since my cousin Ruthie had expertly typed my thesis on it. I bought a typing handbook and commenced to practice eight hours each day for the next three weeks. By the end of that time I could type about forty words a minute, with numerous mistakes and over-strikes, but at least I knew the keyboard. The only job available in the Corps of Engineers at that time was as a clerk at a lower salary than what I had been earning in Washington. My salary was to be $1,260 a year, down from the magnificent sum of $1,440.

Hitler was by now making massive strides across Europe. Where would he go from there?

Here in my own country, things did not look good. The America First Committee had been organized in October 1940. The German American Bund was flourishing. Native fascist and German Nazi groups were rapidly expanding their malevolent anti-Semitic activities. Numerous isolationist newspapers spewed venom through editorials aimed at Roosevelt, who, they said, was intent upon entering the war. Colonel Charles Lindbergh preached passivity and appeasement. Early in 1941, after the Battle of Britain, he said: "This war is lost. It is not within our power today to win the war for England, even though we throw the entire resources of our nation into the conflict." And furthermore, he added, "only the British, the Jews, and the Roosevelt administration" want war. He had been called to Berlin as a consultant to Hitler and had gone eagerly. In spite of the hero's status he enjoyed at home, I saw him as a true, whole-hearted American Nazi. Many Americans listened to his words and believed in what he preached.

Although we American Jews were aware of the fate Hitler was planning for us, most gentiles, especially those in Germany and Austria, pretended they did not know the barbaric inhumanity being enacted against the Jews. I feel certain that on a deep spiritual level, gentiles throughout the world knew; on a conscious level they did not wish to know. They turned their faces away, denied the truth, and openly or tacitly agreed with Hitler. It was a frightening, uncertain time.

John Gunther wrote in *Roosevelt in Retrospect*: "The German Luftwaffe called for planes able to bomb New York as early as 1939. Hitler and the Japanese foreign minister, Maztsuoka, worked out joint plans for attacking the United States on both oceans early in 1941." Their goal was clear. At 1:47 P.M. on Sunday, December 7, 1941, Japan attacked Pearl Harbor, "a day that lives in infamy."

Just prior to Pearl Harbor, I was at work in the War Department in Boston. I had been there only a few months. The east coast was seriously preparing itself for enemy aerial attack. At night it was not possible to venture outdoors without a flashlight. The streets of Boston were as dark and deserted as were those of New York. In fact, the entire east coast had been blacked out. My mother pleaded with me to return home. I suppose she thought that if we were going to die, the family should die together. I was able to arrange a transfer from the Corps of Engineers in Boston to the Corps of Engineers in New York, and I returned home early in 1942. The war against Japan was already at fever pitch; Japan had forced our hand that fateful day in December.

At the U.S. Army Corps of Engineers in New York, I was in charge of six clerks. We were handling classified mail pertaining to bases our country was secretly building at Goose Bay, Greenland, and along the entire North Atlantic coast. It was my job to open all mail pertaining to these fortifications. I would read the incoming letters and assign them code numbers according to subject, so that the letters could easily be retrieved at some later time should this be necessary. Each letter was then summarized by one of my clerks, and the precis put in a file by code number. This done, I routed the letter to the appropriate officer for his attention and action. As the war heated up, we began to work at a frenetic pace, ten hours a day, seven days a week.

In light of the depressing war news and the tremendous power and fervor Germany displayed, I decided I needed to do more for the war effort than to be, by then, a $1,620-a-year supervisory clerk with the War Department. My heart broke for the Jewish people in Germany and Austria, and I truly feared for my people everywhere as well as for myself here at home. Hitler was intent upon destroying us all. We were vermin, he screamed to the world, vermin that must be exterminated. I decided to join the Army, since I was already working for it as a civilian. But the Army refused me a commission; I would have to enlist and come up through the ranks, they said. Yet I knew educated men were being commissioned on the spot. Why not educated women?

So I turned to the Navy. They said they would consider me for a commission, but I would first have to take a written examination. Fair enough. Late in 1942 I took the Navy exam. It turned out to be a battery of exams in English, math, and science.

The Navy Years; World War II _____

I reported to 33 Pine Street in New York, and started my exam at 8:00 A.M. I did not finish until late afternoon. When I handed in my papers, I was ordered to sit in a room with several other people and wait my turn. Soon I was ushered into an inner office, where several Naval officers sat at a long table.

One of the men, obviously the chairman of the committee, stood up as I entered: "We had agreed to accept you for the V-9 officer training program," he said, "but, after discussing your case carefully, we feel you'd be of more service to your country if you remained at Columbia to finish your doctorate. The world will be hungry after this war, and as a botanist, you will be important in helping provide food where and when it is needed."

My heart sank. Were they disqualifying me? "No," I shot back. "I don't agree with you. You see, I am a Jew. There may be no world for me after this war."

The lieutenant, visibly shaken, was silent for a few moments. Then, in a solemn voice, looking me straight in the eye, he said: "Raise your right hand and say after me: "I do solemnly swear to uphold the Constitution of the United States...." Etc., etc.

"Yes, yes, I do," I said, fighting back my tears of joy, of pride, of fear.

On November 18, 1942, I underwent an extensive physical exam by a Navy doctor. I have kept the record of that exam amongst my Navy papers all these years. It reads as follows:

Ruth Ann Bobrov
Date of birth: August 11, 1919
Nationality: W—U.S.
Religion: Hebrew
Ht. 62 $^{1}/_{2}$ inches
Wt. 139
Pulse: 84
Blood Pressure 126/86

Young and strong and willing I was, although I must admit to being a bit overweight.

It was a Saturday, and I was feeling very ill at work. By the time I reached home, I was feverish and coughing hard. Completely exhausted, I crawled into bed. The Sabbath over, my mother and father left for the butcher shop. I remained in bed, alone in the house, dozing, feeling very, very sick.

My parents returned shortly after midnight. Too weak to move, I asked my father to help me to the bathroom. I tried to walk, but lost consciousness and fell to the floor. Papa carried me back to bed.

My Uncle Sam came very early the next morning. I had pneumonia. Apparently the strain of working seven days a week, eight to ten hours a day, was more than my immune system could handle. Also, there was a rumor abroad that a pneumococcus carried by pigeons was responsible for an epidemic of pneumonia in New York that year, 1942. The War Department office, where I worked, was across the street from a small park swarming with pigeons, and I ate my sack lunch there every day, feeding crumbs to the pigeons as they hovered about me. Does one ever know with certainty where one contacts a pathogen?

I was in bed for only a few days when a letter, dated January 5, 1943, arrived from the Navy Department. My heart pounded as I opened the envelope. It was from the director of Naval officer placement. "You are hereby ordered to active

duty with pay and directed to proceed and report to the
Commanding Officer, Smith College, at Northhampton, Massachusetts, on January 16, 1943."

My eyes filled with tears. I had finally received my orders.
I was in! The Navy had accepted me. But I was seriously ill.
Too ill to carry out my orders. Too ill to fight a war. Too ill to
do anything but lie in bed helpless.

I notified the Navy of my illness and was told to inform
them via my physician when I was physically fit for duty. It
took six weeks before my doctor agreed to write such a letter.
My orders to active duty arrived on June 9, 1943.

I did not attend Smith College, where most women officer
candidates on the V-9 program were trained. Instead I was
one of a small group of women who trained at Mt. Holyoke
College, a prestigious women's college in a beautiful rural setting near Pittsfield, Massachusetts. I presume we were the
overflow from the group at Smith.

The next six weeks were very strenuous, both physically
and emotionally. We women marched. We studied late into
the night until curfew ordered us to bed. We learned how to
identify and distinguish the silhouettes of American and foreign ships and aircraft. We studied Navy regulations and were
tested on what we studied. We were inoculated against ty-
phoid and tetanus, and God knows what else. We were indoc-
trinated to hate the Japanese by means of weekly films depict-
ing horrible atrocities committed against Americans by our
slant-eyed enemy.

As for me, I really needed no prodding or further inspiration to remain in the military. For the past several years, I had
been carefully following the newspaper reports of German
atrocities against the Jews. Each Sunday, on my one day off, I
went to the movies in nearby Pittsfield with several other female midshipmen. There we saw newsreels of the rapid and
vicious progress the Nazis were making in Europe. And we
saw abbreviated snippets of German genocide of Jews. It
seemed strange to me that the Navy never showed us any

anti-German propaganda films. Was it too early in the war for my country to realize that the Germans were equally or possibly more malevolent than the Japanese? I felt certain the United States was deliberately avoiding acknowledging the holocaust in progress in Europe. I knew my life and the lives of all Jews everywhere were on the line, and I had more personal fear of the Germans than of the Japanese. While I understood them both to be the enemy, colluding with one another, I wondered why the American government was still unready to recognize how rapacious was the ambition of the Germans under Hitler. Why only anti-Japanese propaganda? This added further to my suspicion of my own government's commitment to fighting the Nazis.

My parents attended my graduation from midshipman's school. Sunday, the 27th of July, 1943, was a beautiful, warm, sunny day. A Navy band played stirring marching music as we women, now commissioned officers in full uniform, proudly paraded to the music while the audience applauded.

The marching over, we were ushered into a large room filled with soft chairs and sofas, there to await further orders. Each of us was to be assigned her specific berth on that day. Excitement ran high as each name was called in turn. I could hardly wait. Finally, I heard, "Bobrov, Ruth Ann." The commanding officer handed me a sealed envelope.

My hands shaking, I tore open the letter: "When directed by your commanding officer and upon execution of the Acceptance and Oath of Office under your commission as Ensign, W-V (S)...U.S.N.R., you will regard yourself detached from all duties at your present station...and you will proceed and report for active duty as indicated below: To Portsmouth, Virginia and the Commandant, Norfolk Navy Yard, for duty, reporting by letter to the Commandant, Fifth Naval District."

I, Ruth Ann Bobrov, at that moment accepted proudly, fiercely, and with absolute certainty, my appointment as ensign in the U.S. Naval Reserve, my first assignment to be the Norfolk Navy Yard, Portsmouth, Virginia.

On that day, the 27th of July, I accompanied my parents back to New York for a few days of leave before reporting to the Navy yard.

With my four shoe coupons which I had been issued, I bought two pairs of shoes, saving two coupons for future use. The shoes I bought were Navy-approved black oxfords with low heels.

On the evening of August 1, 1943, suitcase in hand, I took the subway downtown from the Bronx to Grand Central Station for departure to Portsmouth. I went alone. No fuss, no tears, no fear of the unknown, only determination and great excitement. I was to report for duty on August 2. My directions were to pick up my train reservations at any ticket window at Grand Central Station in Manhattan.

I approached a window. "You have a reservation for me," I said, handing the ticket agent a copy of my orders. "I am on my way to the Norfolk Navy Yard, Portsmouth, Virginia."

The clerk looked up, rifled through a few papers on his desk, and moaned, "Oh, no. Oh, no. You can't be Ensign Bobrov! Oh, no."

"But I am," I replied firmly, sensing some grave error.

"Oh, my God, I've got you in a roomette with a male officer. Oh, my God...."

For a moment I panicked and then quickly regained composure as I realized this was his problem, not mine. After a bit, he seemed to have straightened the matter out, at least to my satisfaction. I was given a handsome, large roomette to myself. I never discovered what happened to the male officer with whom I was expected to share quarters. Never before or since have I traveled in such style on a train.

During my next three years in the Navy, I learned how to live graciously, despite the war. A first-generation American raised in a lower-middle-class neighborhood in the Bronx, I had learned very few social amenities in the first twenty-three years of my life. In the Navy I wore clothes made of fine fabrics, ate excellent non-kosher food, lived in well-furnished quarters, was protected by Marine guards at the gate, had medical care whenever I needed it, and worked very, very hard. I learned a lot about living with others, about sharing, and about giving. And I was willing to work hard. It was my personal war against the Nazis. My life depended upon my own efforts and upon my country being victorious.

In August, 1943, four female Naval Officers, WAVES (Women Appointed for Voluntary Emergency Service), arrived at the Norfolk Navy Yard in Portsmouth, Virginia. In our new uniforms, we made a crisp, sharp appearance. The uniforms were designed by Schiaparelli, the world-famous designer who, at the time of the war, had shops for the wealthy in Paris and London. During the war years she closed down her operations and did not reopen until the war was over in 1945.

The Navy yard was not yet prepared to accept female officers. There were several BOQs (bachelor officer quarters) on base but no WOQs (women officer quarters). We were the first female Naval personnel to arrive in Portsmouth, and we were housed temporarily in an enlisted men's barracks which had been vacated expressly for us. This was a little unnerving because we four women occupied only a very small portion of a huge barracks building designed to house a large number of men. Except for our presence, the two-story building was vacant. The bathroom was a typical male barracks type, no partitions, one huge room with lines of sinks, urinals, toilets, etc. The building was immediately inside the Navy yard gates, in an area normally reserved for enlisted men. Several armed Marines stood guard at the gate twenty-four hours a day. Their presence assuaged our fear a bit, though not entirely. Often we could hear noises in other parts of the building, echoes perhaps originating from activity in neighboring barracks. But sleeping, showering, and dressing in a large, virtually unoccupied building was frightening. Often we would ask a Marine guard to inspect our building, to check for trespassers, or to explain noises we did not understand.

We did not remain in this location long before a warehouse at the other end of the Navy yard was liberated for us. By then, several more female officers had arrived, and we were now a contingent of ten WAVE officers. No enlisted women had yet arrived; they were to come later.

Our new home was a red brick warehouse building, two stories high, just a few yards from the home of Admiral Gygax, commandant of the Navy yard. Partitions were erected in the otherwise open space, forming small rooms. These were our quarters, the WOQ. Each room was furnished with two comfortable beds, a dresser, and an upholstered chair. Two women were to share each room.

It was to the commandant of the Norfolk Navy Yard, Admiral Felix Gygax, that I reported for duty on August 2, 1943. I was ushered into a room with large windows. In front of the windows at a huge desk sat a man in a white shirt, admiral's insignia adorning his open collar.

I saluted: "Ensign Bobrov reporting for duty, sir," I said.

"At ease," he answered, as he stood up. "Welcome aboard."

He leaned over his desk to shake my hand. My jaw dropped. This impressive man was wearing, to my great surprise, a pair of shorts. It was indeed a very hot day but, having just finished studying Navy regs, I was under the impression that no one, not even an officer of his elevated rank, had permission to wear shorts while on duty. Wasn't he out of uniform?

I soon discovered that the humidity in Virginia in the summer was unbearable. Shorts were certainly appropriate. But despite the heat, we officers were still obliged to wear a fully buttoned uniform at all times when outdoors. Indoors we kept electric fans going. These were pre-air conditioner days. When at work, I often pulled off my tie and opened my collar, but I had to keep an eye out for my superior officer, who might be coming down the hall at any moment. Several times I was reprimanded for being out of uniform, that is, not quite conscientious enough about keeping my "blouse" buttoned. (A blouse, in Navy terms, is the outer blue jacket worn over the buttoned white shirt beneath.)

We were permitted whites for summer formal wear and also seersucker cotton uniforms for work in the summer. At a specific time of the year, Admiral Gygax would issue a written order mandating the dress code for the season. Summer uniforms were to be worn from a specified date in May until a specified date in September. Blue winter garb was *de rigueur* from September until further notice. The lighter summer clothing was some relief from the heat and humidity of Virginia, although the white shirt and black tie had to be worn and buttoned at any and all seasons and with any and all uniforms, navy-blue, white, or gray.

I was assigned the duty of assistant personnel officer. My immediate supervisor was Lieutenant Commander Stutts. My fellow personnel officer in the adjoining room was Lt. Gillespie. He was an attorney who had, in civilian life, been mayor of Tazewell, Virginia. He spoke with a soft southern drawl which sounded strange to my northeastern ear. Where was Tazewell, Virginia? I looked it up on the map. It was a town of a few thousand people on the border between Virginia and West Virginia, near Kentucky. I could not believe such a tiny city existed, having come from New York City with its millions of people. So, from him, for the first time in my life, I learned something about small towns and the mind-set of the people who inhabit them. My education began to expand.

For a twenty-three-year-old unsophisticated, inexperienced woman from the Bronx, I carried a lot of responsibility. It was my job to interview civilian workers who might have a complaint against the Navy yard, or who, dissatisfied for one reason or another, might want to quit to seek work elsewhere. It was my duty to handle the workers' complaints, and I took my job seriously. Actually, it was my responsibility to attempt to bar any civilian from leaving the Navy yard except for the most compelling of reasons. Work on the ships had to progress! I had been trained as a scientist, not as a social worker. The only prerequisite I needed for this job was to have heart—miles and miles and miles of it.

Most of the people I interviewed were black. To be black in Virginia in those days was indeed dire. I was a north-easterner, unaccustomed to and unaccepting of the blatant anti-black prejudice I was encountering in the South. While as a Jew I was familiar with the concept of prejudice, southern feeling against blacks was, if possible, even more pernicious.

After a few weeks at work, I requested permission from Admiral Gygax to have a room of my own in the WOQ. He granted my request. Since I worked hard interviewing people all day, I felt a need for my own quiet space away from others. I moved my sea chest into my room, made a pretty gray cloth cover for it, and hung several pictures on the walls. Marines stood guard at the main gate just outside the WOQ day and night. I felt very comfortable, very well protected. I was ready to do the best job I could.

The Navy yard was a bustling place. Work went on night and day building aircraft carriers known as flattops and repairing the war-damaged ships of our own and of friendly nations which limped into our yard. Much of the workforce was female. The civilian lunchroom was noisy and overcrowded. On occasion, I took lunch there. It kept me in touch with the people whose problems it was my job to understand, address, or redress. More often I ate lunch at the officers' club, where the food was far superior.

The civilian lunchroom was a greasy-spoon type restaurant. The food swam in fat. Perhaps the rationale for this type of cooking was that laborers needed a large number of calories in order to carry on heavy work. But more probably this was traditional Southern-style cooking to which I was unaccustomed. The civilians, male and female, worked hard, plumbers, riveters, pipe-fitters, painters, and carpenters. The expression "Rosie the Riveter" must have originated in the

Navy yards of America. Acetylene torches blazed away day and night aboard ships we were building from scratch and those bomb-damaged ships we were repairing.

I interviewed approximately thirty to forty civilians a day. I no sooner arrived at my office at 0800 hours than the day's work began. Already the reception room was full of people, anxiously waiting to see me, to talk, to unburden, to request something or other. Each officer had a coffee pot steaming away in his or her office. I would throw my hat on the hat tree in the corner, pull off my tie, cast an eye on the pile of complaints on my desk, walk out to the front reception room and call the first name on the pile. "Jones, Henry...."

My office was one of several in a wooden barracks building. Flimsy partitions separated one tiny office from another. Mine was the first cubicle beyond the reception room. The windows were behind me as I sat. I had a desk, a desk chair for myself, and a chair for the complainant. Also a hat tree. That was all of it! On the wall to my right, to cover the coarse, unpainted plywood separating me from the neighboring cubicle, I pinned up a huge National Geographic map of the United States, my country.

I felt as if I alone were responsible for winning the war. I still have a small tray which the foreman of the woodworking shop, Doc Williams, carved for me from the mahogany door of a captured German battleship. The Germans had converted this ship from one of their prewar elegant cruise liners to a war vessel. Our Navy captured this one and was dismantling it. We could salvage the parts and reuse them. Doc Williams thought I would like a souvenir. He understood my anti-German zeal; I made no secret of it.

Most of the people I interviewed were African-American males. Occasionally I saw a woman. Since almost all physically able, literate, black or white men were already conscripted and in the armed forces, those who remained behind were either illiterate or physically disabled, and thus ineligible for military service. The Civil Service Commission, in conjunction with the Navy, beat the bushes for men who were still at home and who could be of some use in building ships. We needed manpower. In the small towns of Virginia, West Virginia, and North and South Carolina, many black men were discovered who couldn't read or write. We could use them. Some few were 4F. We could use them, too. We brought these people to Portsmouth to train for relatively low-level but nevertheless essential work in the building of ships. Skilled workers were mainly white, exempted from military service because their labor was deemed essential to the war effort. We had almost as many women laborers as men.

The Navy built long one-story wooden buildings to house the black men we had recruited. It was adequate housing with good plumbing, although, to be truthful, it afforded the men relatively little privacy. Each man had a small room for himself and his few possessions. Several months after the men were moved in, I, as one of the members of a committee of Naval officers ordered to inspect civilian quarters, found toilets that had been smashed as if with hammers, garbage strewn everywhere, and the buildings and walls in shambles. From interviewing hundreds of these men, I had become keenly aware of the anger seething in them at what life had dealt them. This was a black backlash or, more aptly, blacklash.

On occasion I would take the civilian bus into Portsmouth. I was astonished to see black people queue up to wait for whites to board first. In the north I had never encountered such behavior. I was not so naive as to believe prejudice did not exist in the north, but nothing approached the rude, unfeeling discrimination of the Southern whites. When I first arrived in Virginia, I would stand aside and wait for those who had arrived first to board, black or white. But the whites always entered first; the black people stood mutely aside. At first, I continued to wait. After you, Alphonse, I would think, motioning the black person to board. But finally I found it was no joking matter. This was serious stuff, and there was no bucking the system. In addition, after they finally got on board, blacks were obliged to move to the back of the bus. I was so disturbed by this that I rarely went into town except on foot or by Navy bus, where civilian rules did not apply.

In the Navy yard, on Navy turf, I had a little more control of Southern discriminatory practice, although not as much as I would have liked. When I thought a person, black or white, had a legitimate complaint against his foreman or his shop supervisor, I would grab my hat from the rack, button my blouse, tie my tie, and proceed with the person in tow to the shop. I soon found that very little could be done to buck southern anti-black feeling. It may be that by my efforts a few blacks were helped temporarily, but I was powerless to make any real change in the prevailing attitude. The time for Afro-American equality had not yet arrived...but it clearly needed coming.

On many occasions a black interviewee would complain of illness. With my limited knowledge of medicine, I could diagnose (without certainty) the symptoms of venereal disease or tuberculosis or heart disease. Such people I sent to the medical office, where a Navy doctor would ascertain his ailment and recommend how I was to proceed. I was the officer in charge of dispensing Statements of Availability. If I issued such a statement, the person was permitted to leave the Navy yard workforce to seek work elsewhere. Without such a statement he was, by law, unemployable elsewhere in any occupation or industry in the United States. With the war raging, I could not permit many workers to leave, except those who were gravely ill or had some other compelling personal reason.

One black man I interviewed pleaded for release. He was 4F, a graduate of Ohio State University. He said he had come south to work, to see for himself how his people were being treated. He found life in the South intolerable and appeared to be in great emotional distress. I agreed to give him a Statement of Availability so he could return to the north, but cautioned him to seek work in a war-related industry.

Aside from the hectic, frenetic pace at the Norfolk Navy Yard, my work as a Naval officer was interesting and rewarding. Early in my assignment, I met and became close friends with Lt. Bill Atkinson, a Texan. He was ship superintendent, overseeing construction of the *Shangri-La* (CV 38), our then newest flattop. We came to know one another well because it was I who interviewed many of the civilians who were building his ship. He needed the people I was interviewing.

Bill was a jovial person, hail-fellow-well-met. He had been a highly trained, experienced engineer in civilian life. In Amarillo, Texas, his hometown, he had left behind his job, a wife, and six children.

Bill and I hit it off immediately. Come 4:30 P.M., after the waiting room thinned out, my day's work done and my mind tired and craving rest, Bill and I were off to the officers' club for an early dinner. Or we might attend the enlisted men's mess at the opposite end of the Navy yard. The food was adequate in both places, although the officers' mess was a lot less plebeian and a lot more expensive. Also at the officers' club one could order alcoholic beverages with one's meal; this was *verboten* at the enlisted men's mess. Bill was a heavy drinker but he was willing, at my request, to forego the booze when with me. I, a consummate teetotaler, was a sort of Carrie Nation in the officers' club, constantly trying to persuade the men to stop drinking. I soon learned I couldn't fight the bottle. The men were drinking to drown out the uncertainty of life or, at least, being in the Navy provided them a good excuse. I am sure many of them were confirmed alcoholics long before they joined the Navy.

Sometimes, after dinner, Bill and I would stop at a small cafe in town for a cup of coffee. He smoked huge, smelly cigars and, as we sat lingering over our coffee, we listened to the jukebox playing "Begin the Beguine" or "I'll Be Seeing You." When I hear those old songs today, I have flashbacks to the unpretentious little cafe where he and I sat in semi-darkness and quietude while the war-crazed world outside rushed on without us for a few brief moments.

One evening after dinner we walked out the back gate of the Navy yard and continued walking for miles, deeply engrossed in conversation. The sun was just beginning to set. We put war work behind us as we walked and chatted. It seemed as if we were alone in a vast forgotten space, where nothing could touch us. The streets were empty. Not a soul was stirring.

We approached a bridge and started across it when, at that very moment, a barge came tooting along. The bridge, probably automatically triggered by the barge, started to lift from the middle, the two halves slowly rising higher and higher in the air. We clung to the guardrails and to one another, hearts racing. When the barge finally passed, the two halves of the bridge began to descend, ever so slowly. I remember my terror. Would we come out of this alive? Life had taken on a strange patina. Anything might happen, because almost everything did happen! We were not in control; none of us in those days were sure of anything. When the bridge returned to its normal horizontal position, we stood in the glow of the sunset, holding tight to one another. We laughed and laughed at having defied death. We were so happy to be alive.

Bill finally finished his job as ship superintendent of the *Shangri-La.* On February 24, 1944, the flattop was ready to be launched and make her maiden voyage. And Bill would be going out with her.

It is interesting how this ship came to bear its name. On April 18, 1942, Lt. Col. James Doolittle led a bomber raid against Tokyo. This was the very first time Army bombers had taken off from a Navy aircraft to fly such a long distance, 800 miles, and in such numbers. Information about the raid was kept top secret; very few Naval officers or government officials knew anything about this attack. Later, at a press conference, President Roosevelt was questioned about the mission.

Where had the planes taken off from, he was asked. Tongue-in-cheek he answered: "They took off from a secret base in Shangri-La." Actually, the planes had taken off from the USS *Hornet*, which unfortunately, was later lost in battle. That was the way, thanks to Roosevelt, the flattop *Shangri-La* got its name.

James Hilton was expected to christen *Shangri-La* by breaking the bottle of champagne across her prow. This seemed appropriate, since it was he who had created the fictional land, Shangri-La, in his book *Lost Horizon*. But for some reason, at the very last moment, he could not come. Instead, Mrs. James Doolittle was the substitute sponsor. She tried again and again to break the bottle against the prow, and finally she succeeded. Everybody cheering, the beautiful, sleek, powerful ship slipped smoothly, proudly into the Atlantic. Tears streamed down my face as I wished her and Bill "Happy hunting; safe return!"

With the country at war, sexual behavior was free and open in the Navy, if one chose it. This was undoubtedly true in the Army and Marine Corps as well. Men, feeling their lives were precarious and fleeting, threw caution and so-called "sexual morality" to the wind. Scuttlebutt had it that the women in the military were sexually loose. But this was no more true of women than of men. Sex was easily available to both genders, since they were thrown so closely together. As a woman, I knew I needed to keep my wits about me, and I did. Regaled on all sides by men just about to depart on warships off to battle, it was difficult for military women to remain uninvolved. But neither did women outside the military remain uninvolved, although they may have had less proximity to military men than we military women had. Male sexual exploits were taken for granted and were not openly condemned, as were those of women. But in both military service and in civilian life, both sexes were, in their anxiety, "acting out."

While at the Navy yard, I started to correspond with Ronald Cramer, the brother of my friend Harriet, with whom I had kept in contact from the time we were children together in the Bronx. Ronald had graduated from dental school and was now a captain in the Air Force at McCarran Air Force Base in Las Vegas, Nevada. Harriet urged me to write to him, and I did.

Emotions, as I have said, ran high in those days. Life was on the line. I saw our warships and those of friendly nations come into port, disabled, shattered, huge gaping holes in their sides from enemy bombs. It seemed as if ships of the entire friendly world had descended upon the Norfolk Navy Yard for help—British, Australian, Peruvian, Russian. How many lives had been lost? And who in the American military, man or woman, felt certain of a tomorrow?

The environment was very heady. I wrote to Ronald with passion, although I barely knew him. He wrote back with somewhat less ardor, although enough to excite me. Often he would phone me at the WOQ. Each time the phone rang in the hall, I would listen breathlessly. Was this call for me, from Ron? In hindsight, which is always so clear, I understand how foolish, how unfounded our relationship was. I had never been alone with this man. I had no knowledge of his personality. I did not know what he liked, how he thought, or what his hopes and aspirations were. In truth, I did not even remember how he looked.

From Ronald's point of view, our relationship was equally irrational. He knew no more of me than I of him. When, via mail, he proposed marriage, I committed myself to be his wife. Having done this, I felt some small relief in the face of the crazy sexual scene at the Navy yard.

Ronald and I planned to be married in Los Angeles in April, 1944. We both requested a week's leave, I from the Norfolk Navy Yard, he from McCarran Air Force Base in Nevada. My mother met me in Portsmouth. Together we took the train west. It took over three days to make the tedious journey. As we sat in the train, moving ever closer to our destination, I embroidered bathroom hand-towels, small cherries on a white background. I dreamed of peace, a home, domestic responsibilities, and children. That is what my parents had told me to want. A Jewish girl got married, preferably to a doctor, her career (if she dared to have one) ended, and domesticity began. She took care of home and husband, saw that his career flourished, and prepared to have and care for children. Husband and wife then lived happily together 'til death did them part. There was no strain, no pain, and no disagreement. It was all quite beautiful.

As the train chugged across the wide-open plains of America, I did not contemplate anything negative about marriage. In the strange upside-down world in which we were living, with an uncertain future, possibly no future, I completely romanticized marriage. *Verborgen*, buried, were my dreams of being a research scientist. Looking back through the years I wonder how I could have embarked on such a strange journey. At twenty-four years of age I had never yet had a meaningful sexual relationship. And I knew myself to be mortally afraid of sex. Yet here I was crossing the country from Virginia to California to enter into union with a man I barely knew. Somewhere in that part of my mind in which some small degree of rationality still existed, a quiet voice told me I was making a huge mistake.

The train was now fast approaching Los Angeles. I had never before been west of Kansas City, where I had once visited my paternal family. That morning I awoke early, pulled up the green shade, and, from my upper berth, looked out on a forest of Joshua trees. This was a vast, desolate country, at once frightening and fascinating. The trees looked like giants standing guard over the world, their huge arms projecting in all directions. The southwestern desert, which I had never seen before, was an awesome sight.

I was beginning to get the jitters. In a few hours I would

be meeting the man I was going to marry. Writing letters across the country was one thing; facing the real thing was quite another. I could not stop shaking.

We were married in the Religious Conference Building at UCLA by Rabbi Harrison, the Hillel rabbi, a Reform Jew. It was an inauspicious affair. We were both in uniform. The rabbi, who had never seen either of us before, spoke a few generic, meaningless words. Following the ceremony Ron's immediate family, my mother and I, and a few of the Cramers' cousins went to a restaurant for lunch.

I sat to one side of my new husband. On the other side sat his cousin Flora, whom I had never met before nor would ever see again. She was a tall, willowy young woman, about my age, very pretty and vivacious—just the opposite of how I saw myself. In my head, I was still Solly's kid sister, the "fat horse," chubby, intense, intellectual. Ron, seemingly disinterested in me, spent his time flirting with Flora. Again I had the uneasy feeling that I had made a serious error. But it was too soon for me to accept defeat. I could sense my mother's silent disapproval. Perhaps she intuited my distress, but she said nothing. That was her cold way. The following day she took the train back to New York. That night Ron and I flew to Las Vegas, where my new husband had made reservations for our honeymoon at the El Rancho Motel. We arrived late in the night.

In anticipation of my wedding night, I had purchased an elegant nightgown in Norfolk. I fantasized my wedding night would be a beautiful experience. I disrobed in the bathroom and slipped into my lovely, lace-trimmed gown. If Ron were interested, he didn't show it. He made no comment about my gown or anything else. In bed we tried to make love, but nothing flowed. After an hour or so of half-hearted trying, we turned away from one another and went to sleep back to back. I was happy when, a few days later, I boarded the train to return to my work at the Navy yard, still refusing to admit to myself I had made a huge blunder. Ron returned to his base at the outskirts of Las Vegas, probably as happy to be rid of me as I was of him.

Now, so many years later, I think back on those years when I made the decision to marry Ronald and wonder how I could have lost track of the academic dream I had held so close to my heart prior to the war. Through the mist of time I remember that each day the war raged on my prewar dreams of an academic future receded further from reality. They were of another life in another world, one that might never again be. In the heat of war, in the confused frenzy of my life at the time, there seemed to be no future, only the moment. And I had mindlessly seized the moment. I never really loved Ron.

I returned to the Navy yard a married woman. I had achieved the goal for which all nice Jewish girls strive—at least the goal my parents had set for me. I had married a doctor, or rather, a dentist, which was almost as good. I had met all the prerequisites for acceptance into Jewish marry-dom, except I was miserable. Still leading with my head, I paid no attention to my heart which silently cried, "Abort this damned marriage." Instead, I requested transfer to the west coast. That would bring me closer to Ronald. Married people were supposed to be close to one another, were they not? Maybe I could make marriage work yet. I knew that at war's end, if we were still married, we would settle in Los Angeles, where Ron's family lived. If nothing else, I had stumbled on a way to escape New York.

In December 1944, my request for a transfer was granted. Eight months after my wedding, in a torrential downpour, I arrived by Greyhound bus at Camp Parks in Pleasanton, California, just north of Hayward. My berth was communications officer at the Naval Construction Battalion (CB) base. I was in charge of the Navy post office. I had some seventy enlisted personnel under me, mostly men, a few women.

Our WOQ at Camp Parks was elegant. It was brand new, a low, rambling redwood building with lovely large bedrooms, tastefully furnished. The officers' club was equally elegant, in

the same decor. The entire base was quite new, set in the bosom of the low rolling hills of the Livermore Valley, very pastoral, very peaceful. The base's *raison d'etre* was as a receiv-
ing station for battalions of men returning from overseas and
to re-form those battalions to ship out as replacement contin-
gents. In charge of the post office, it was my duty to distribute
incoming mail to the personnel on base as well as to make
certain that mail expeditiously reached the men who had just
been shipped out. Mail was very important to the morale of
military people, especially those overseas.

I did not enjoy this job as much as I had the one at Portsmouth, but I had asked for transfer to California, and there I
was. I changed my legal residence from New York to California and knew the rest of my life would be spent in the southwest. And indeed it has been.

My immediate superior officer was Lt. Waters. We disliked each other on sight. However, the man with whom I was
to have most contact was a chief petty officer by the name of
Tyler, an inveterate alcoholic.

Most of the Navy drank heavily; Tyler was no exception. I
vividly recalled the words of the Yiddish ditty my father had
taught me as a tot:

> *Schiker is er*
> *Trinken muss er*
> *Veil er is a goy-oy-oy.*

When I was small, I would sing this song in Yiddish, much
to the delight of my adult relatives, who would laugh and clap
for me. But I didn't know then what the words meant; I was
just being cute. Actually, the song inferred that all Christians
were compulsive drinkers, whereas Jews were always clean
and sober. Now the ditty kept repeating itself in my teetotaler
head. Here in the middle of my war was a longtime addicted,
falling-down drunk. And he was my right-hand man! This was
no way to win the war.

Tyler was a tall, handsome, well-built gentile, very intelligent when sober. But it took him half the morning to come out of his nightly drunken stupor. *"Trinken muss er!"* I had no tolerance for his habit.

At first, I spoke calmly with him, explaining I would not tolerate his being drunk or hungover on the job. I repeated this time and again, growing more frustrated each time. Then I pleaded. Then I shouted. In desperation, I threatened to have him shipped overseas if he did not appear at the post office sober at 0800 hours every morning. Nothing availed. I had no knowledge then that his drinking was more an illness than a simple habit easily broken should he wish it. He obviously felt that he could not handle his life without the help of alcohol, which was readily available. Nights were long and empty. What better for an addicted alcoholic than to drink himself into oblivion each night?

Yet he was my chief petty officer. He was the only person who had the combination to the safe in which we kept approximately $6,000 in stamps and money orders. Nobody else, including me, had access to it. When he didn't show up at 0800, I and my entire crew stood around waiting helplessly, unable to start the day's work. Sailors began to line up for stamps and money orders, and the lines grew longer as we all waited impatiently; I grew more tense with each passing minute. Every morning Tyler arrived late, wobbly, unable to shake himself out of his stupor. Every morning I feared that perhaps this time he had gone AWOL and absconded with the money from the safe. And I had this vision with good reason.

At the Norfolk Navy Yard, just before my departure, a fellow lieutenant had been given a court martial for a crime of which he was innocent. He was the fiscal officer on base. One of the enlisted men under his command had stolen several thousand dollars. The thief was apprehended and jailed, but his officer was also brought to trial. That was the Navy way. Although the crime had not been committed by him, he, as the officer in charge, bore equal responsibility for the crime of one of his men. The enlisted man was thrown into the brig; the officer was severely reprimanded but not incarcerated. A few weeks later, the officer died of a massive heart attack. This incident had made a deep impression on me. I envisioned Tyler stealing money from the safe and absconding, and I, as his immediate supervisor, being held responsible. When Tyler did not yield to my pleas, I finally went topside, where overseas battalions were formed, and arranged to have him transferred to a battalion that was readying to move to Alaska within the week. For doing what I considered my duty, I was severely reprimanded by Lt. Waters, who himself spent every night drinking. From then on, I was openly shunned by the men under my command. The post office became hell.

Even had the Tyler episode not occurred, enlisted men did not like having a female officer in a position of superiority. But they had, until then, tolerated me with more or less good humor and much joshing. Following Tyler's shipment, however, their hostility became open and more intense each day.

It was the rule at Camp Parks that each officer in rotation take a turn standing duty as OOD, officer of the day. This meant that for twenty-four hours he or she was in total command of the post. One Sunday, shortly after the Tyler incident, it was my turn.

It was an uneventful, quiet day on base. At about 2300 hours, my duty only one hour from complete, I decided to return to my quarters. All seemed in order. I could easily be reached were I needed.

The phone rang in the hall. I ran to answer it. A male voice said: "Lt. Cramer?"

"Yes," I answered.

"A coded secret message has been received by the communications office in San Bruno. It was meant for Camp Parks, but was routed here by mistake. It is to be picked up immediately." Before I could ask the voice to identify himself, click, the phone was dead.

It was a dilemma. Camp Parks' secret-coded messages were always received by Camp Shoemaker, adjacent to Camp Parks, about one half mile up the road. That is where I, as communications officer, had always picked up such messages. It was strange that a secret message should be coming in from San Bruno, approximately fifty miles away, and so late at night. Why had it not been sent to Shoemaker in the usual manner?

It was thirty minutes short of 2400 hours, when my duty as OOD would end. Was I to ignore the message? If I did, I ran the risk of being charged with dereliction of duty. Was I to travel the fifty miles? That did not make sense. Not at that hour; not at any hour. I had nobody from whom to seek advice. I alone was in charge.

I decided against going, taking the risk of countermanding an order. I knew the men under my command were angry with me. This could well be a ruse to get me off base, to harm me in some way, or simply to discommode me and send me on a wild goose chase in the middle of the night. If the call were legitimate, I reasoned, the coded message would certainly have been sent through normal channels from San Bruno to Camp Shoemaker, and I would have received the call from Shoemaker. I followed my intuition. I did not go that night. Instead I kept myself awake worrying. As it turned out, I never heard another word about San Bruno's message, not the next day, not ever. My intuition was obviously on target.

Early in May 1945, I received a letter. It was addressed in my own handwriting to: Capt. S. Arthur Bobrov 047770, Medical Detachment 169 Infantry 43rd, A.P.O. 43, c/o Postmaster, San Francisco, Calif.

At first glance I thought testily, what in the world is this? Why is my mail, so clearly addressed to my brother, being sent to me? Such inefficiency! And then I saw that the address was slashed through and, in the left-hand corner of the envelope was stamped the single word DECEASED.

I did not believe my eyes. It was certainly a mistake. In shock, I rushed to a phone to call my parents. Some weeks before they had also had a letter returned to them, they said. In April Solly's wife had been notified by the Army of her husband's death.

Hysterical, I screamed into the phone: "Why didn't you let me know? Why did you let me find out this way?"

Sobbing, my mother said: "We wanted to spare you."

As if one should or could be spared such a reality! But that was my mother's way. It had always infuriated me. Why did she think she could always take charge, even at a miserable moment like this? Was she protecting me—or again controlling me?

Solly had been a dentist in the medical detachment of the 169th Infantry, 43rd Division. He was killed in action in Luzon on March 22, 1945. Although the Philippines had been secured by that time, small pockets of Japanese resistance still remained. It was during mopping up that he was killed, an enemy bullet through the heart.

Torn by grief, I requested leave and took a commercial plane to New York. No military plane was available at the moment.

An aside: I did not think anything could make me smile at such a tragic time, but a comic incident occurred as the prop plane made its way noisily, unsteadily east. With anguished tears streaming down my face, I could not help laughing aloud as two young Army Air Force officers seated across the cabin from me were puking into their air sickness bags. It was a bumpy ride, true, but United States Air Force officers puking? I laughed joylessly, *schadenlachter*. The enemy need not worry if our Air Force officers could not hold their own while on peaceful flights, let alone bombing missions!

Then my mind went back to the last time I had seen my brother.

The phone rings in the WOQ at the Norfolk Navy Yard. It

is Solly calling from an Army base in North Carolina. He has received notice that his unit is imminently to ship out. He does not know where or when, but this weekend is to be his last in the States.

"Meet me in Richmond, kid," he says.

"Sure thing," I answer. "Do you know where you are going?"

"No," he replies, "but we can spend a day or so together. Make reservations in Richmond for Saturday night, will you?"

"I'll try. If I can't find a room, we'll sleep on the street," I laugh halfheartedly.

Hotel rooms are difficult to come by during the war. At such short notice all I can find is a single room with two beds in a dingy hotel in a poor part of town. A bedroom with no bath is as good as I can do.

I take the Greyhound to Richmond. We meet on Saturday and walk the streets all day, talking, absorbed in one another, remembering old times, and making plans for happier times to come at war's end. He will then be able to be a good husband to Suki and a good father to his infant daughter, Leslie, whom he has seen only once just after her birth. He is very excited about shipping out. Unknown places fascinate him. He has always been a daredevil. I remind him of the time he led a bunch of kids to the top of the silo on the farm in Keyserike and, show-off that he was, jumped the full length into a pile of hay below and broke his leg. Solly didn't seem to understand fear.

"And when this is over, Ruthie, you can go to California, finish your doctorate, and have a good life with Ron," he says.

We walk for hours. I am aware that people are looking at us with interest—I, a J.G. in my dress Navy whites and he, so handsome, in his Army captain's uniform and a chest full of medals. We probably look striking together. We sort of epitomize the war effort: Army and Navy bravely facing the enemy.

We stop at an officers' club for a brief bite to eat in the evening. We spend the night together in the shabby hotel room in Richmond. *We laugh and cry together. We do not know when or if we will see one another again. That is the uneasy feeling common to all of us in the military. Something terrible might happen. We pray it will not. But it might. It just might. It is a crap shoot.*

I feel a surge of love for this person with whom I have shared my entire young life. He is my closest blood relative, my only sibling, genetically, biologically, the closest person in the world to me. I forgive him his teasing when we were children, his calling me a fat horse, a klutz, his locking me in the back bedroom when he had parties. Big deal!

"Do you remember that Fourth of July when we were kids and you dropped a 'torpedo' from the roof just as I was coming home? It exploded at my feet and a piece of shrapnel hit me in the leg. God, how that hurt! I still have the scar. You've always been a rascal. Now you're playing with real explosives. Be careful," I caution.

The next morning, after a restless night, we tearfully take leave of one another and start back to our respective bases.

That was the last time I saw Solly.

The plane landed at La Guardia Field in New York. I arrived home to grief. My parents looked gray and drawn. There was nowhere for them to hide from the tragedy. No escape. Nothing to do but to stand still and let life pummel away.

As for me, I could not control my anguish. A continuous sharp pain in the left side of my chest would not leave. My breathing was shallow and irregular. I remembered the words of Admiral Gygax when I had first reported for duty to the Norfolk Navy Yard in August of '43. "You are now Navy property. If you are sick, report to sick bay immediately. If you are in trouble, report to the OOD. Whatever you do from now on reflects on the United States Navy. It is your obligation to keep that reputation unblemished." I called the Navy office on Pine Street and reported my symptoms. "Report in at once," a voice said.

When I arrived at Pine Street, the doctor put a stetho-
scope to my heart and immediately ordered a jeep to drive me
to the Brooklyn Navy Yard hospital. There I remained for two
weeks. Diagnosis: possible heart attack. Solly had been shot
through the heart. The diagnosis was appropriate.

I returned to Camp Parks after my release from the hospital. I had no further desire to help with the war effort. Instead, I felt an overwhelming need to help my parents. I requested release from active duty. The war with Germany was
over. VE day had been declared on May 7, 1945. Japan was
already on her knees. By August, following the second atomic
bombing, she too surrendered. The remaining job for the
military was to mop up the hot spots and disband the troops.
The Navy could do without me; I felt my parents could not.

I was released from duty on September 6, 1945, my discharge to be effective October 3, 1945. I had spent two years
and four months in the service of my country. True, I had lost
Solly, but I had won the war. Germany and Japan were both
defeated, and I knew I had done my best to help achieve the
victory.

Meanwhile, Ronald had been transferred to Sheppard
Field, Wichita Falls, Texas. I went there to await his imminent
discharge before we returned to California. The Air Force,
along with all the military, was moving rapidly to return its
forces to civilian life. I went to Texas to gather my thoughts
and my energy, to salvage whatever could be salvaged, and to
discard whatever could not.

My parents. Above, New York, 1910; left, my father and maternal grandfather, 1926; right, my parents, Papa holding giant squash, Los Angeles, 1946.

My younger days.
Above, my brother, age
7, and I, age 2;
right, Ruth age 7,
second grade.

Above: Ruth in the Navy, 1943
Left: Dr. Orda Plunket, 1949
Right: Dr. Flora Murray Scott,
1951

Clockwise from top: Ph.D. graduation at the Hollywood Bowl, 1951; with Jack Lemon, UCLA, 1970; with Luis Hernandez at his wedding, in Downey, 1974.

Postwar Years—University Career or Marriage?

Texas was completely different from New York, where I had been raised. Not many Jews lived in Wichita Falls in 1945, and I had the uneasy feeling that Texans had not yet accepted the fact that the hatred of Jews was *declassé*.

I arrived there in September 1945, my discharge not yet having taken effect. I owned no civilian clothes, so, still in uniform, I went to the bank to open an account and faced an unexpected inquisition. Previous banks I had known asked the usual questions necessary for security purposes: birthdate, mother's maiden name, social security number, etc. Never before when opening an account anywhere had I been asked my religion. My temper flared. I had just finished fighting a war over that very issue. "What business is that of yours?" I snapped. "I am a Jew." The clerk flushed but did not apologize.

Ron was granted permission to live off base until his imminent release. We rented a tiny house in back of a large mansion. Everything in Texas was big, except our miniature house; it must have been slave quarters at one time.

I found a seamstress to alter my uniforms so they resembled civilian suits. I had her change the gold G.I. buttons to colored, decorative ones. Then I bought a few feminine blouses to replace the mannish white shirts I had been wearing. We bought a few pots and pans. Friends presented us a gift of some clear glass dishes, and we set up temporary housekeeping.

I have a few interesting memories of my short Texas stay. One is of the park. Wichita Falls in 1945 was quite rural. The park, with its many mature pecan trees, was in the middle of town. It was fun to walk through the park with a paper bag picking up pecans that had dropped to the ground. Thin-shelled and easy to crack, they were not only delicious but free for the taking!

I remember torrential rain storms that suddenly arrived out of nowhere. Pouring down, driven by heavy winds, the rain blew through the cracks under the doors and windows of our tiny, poorly insulated house. Several times we were badly inundated as the rain forced its way under the kitchen door and through the loosely fitting windows.

On occasion it would snow, but meagerly. The snow came down for a few minutes, just barely making the ground a fuzzy-white. Then the sun came forth in full glory. It was fun to go outdoors after one of those snow storms with no sweater on, snow underfoot, sun overhead.

There were even a few fun-filled moments with Ron as we tried to become better acquainted. One day we went to see *State Fair*, a movie being shown on base at Sheppard Field. Admission: ten cents! After that we walked down Main Street in town, arm in arm, singing, "I'm as restless as a willow in a windstorm," and "It's a grand night for singing, the moon is flying high." The movie was a total escape from battleships, battalions, service personnel, war, and death. For a brief moment I felt I might just possibly be able to experience the blissful, lighthearted, carefree domesticity that Rodgers and Hammerstein had so poignantly portrayed in their story. With God's help, I thought, perhaps this marriage might work. The good feeling, however, did not last.

A few months after I arrived in Texas, Ron was released from the Air Force and we were free to drive west across the country to Los Angeles, our new home to be. We bought a car, a 1938 Ford two-seater replete with rumble seat. I had no confidence in this old hulk, but it was all we could afford.

New cars were still unavailable; all our country's steel had gone to war-related industries rather than to automobile manufacturing. The Ford cost us $650, just about all the money we had between us.

Our trip from Texas to California was uneventful. Surprisingly, the car behaved. But the heat as we crossed the Arizona desert was unbearable. We had to stop from time to time under the shade of a palo verde tree or at a roadside cafe to cool off. But we made it, singing most of the way, "California, here I come...." We followed the twisting and turning Route 66, two lanes most of its length, all the way to Los Angeles.

The Army had graciously packed all our meager domestic belongings—pots, pans, dishes, and silverware. When we got to California, I discovered that everything had simply been thrown into several large cartons without wrapping or insulation of any sort. All our glasses and dishes were a mass of shards; not one breakable item had survived. It didn't pay to argue the matter with the Army. I was glad to be away from the military.

In Los Angeles, we moved into the adjoining half of the small duplex in which Ronald's parents lived on 39th Place. The rent was minimal. It was a good place to squat until we could adjust to civilian life, find more suitable quarters, and make plans for the future. We slept on a Murphy bed in the dining room. There was a built-in table and benches in the kitchen. Aside from those we had no furniture.

I loved the first set of dishes we bought. For a while, I mourned the demise of the antique clear glass dishes, which our friends had given us in Texas. I replaced them with a colorful set of Bauer dishes. They were crude pottery, brazen colored, manufactured in Pasadena. I loved their happy fiesta colors—yellow, blue, orange, green, and purple. Only the green mixing bowls remain, chipped from years of hard service, but still usable. Today, had I kept them, the dishes would be quite valuable because Bauer closed its doors shortly after the war, and what is left of their pottery is now considered collectible.

Living next door to Ron's family afforded me a good opportunity to observe the personality of the man I had married. I liked little of what I saw. He was fanatically attached to his mother, who never ceased to play the victim role. After the death of her oldest daughter in the distant past, Helen had taken to her couch and rarely left it. I remember her from my youth as always lying on the couch. She was not a good housekeeper. Her meals were plain and dull. However, I remember that she made one dish well; it was rice pudding, the family staple, and she made it again and again. As soon as one batch was consumed, she made another.

Ron was her protector, her savior, and her surrogate husband. Almost every week, he would bring her flowers. His excessive attachment to Mama disturbed me. John, Ron's father, was a free-lance accountant. He made a poor living at best but, in spite of this, he always seemed upbeat. He was a handsome, jovial man who paid little attention to his wife and her unrelenting depression. Ron, on the other hand, paid inordinate attention to each of her complaints.

In spite of my foreboding that my marriage would not last, Ron and I searched up and down the neighborhoods in Los Angeles for a likely place for him to open a dental practice. We purchased a twenty-five-foot piece of land fronting on Western Avenue on which a very small stucco building had been erected. We felt it might serve as a dental office until such time as we could afford something larger.

My brother's dental equipment had been stored in a New York warehouse just before he had gone off to war. He had hoped to use it upon his return. When Ron opened his office, we had the equipment flown from New York to Los Angeles. Solly would have no use for it ever again.

Flying Tigers, an air transport company, was just starting up at the time. The new company had been formed by a group of young pilots just released from Chennault's Flying Tigers, which had been operating in Burma, Thailand, and

China during the war. With their expert help, Solly's equipment arrived in good time and excellent condition. We had it installed in Ron's new office. Ron was ready to begin his practice. At first I worked side by side with him as his assistant-receptionist-bookkeeper, hating every minute of it. Our personalities clashed. Sparks flew. We were totally incompatible.

After we were more or less settled in a small house near the office, I decided to relocate my parents from New York, where memories of my brother continued to haunt them. Starting a new life on the west coast, near me, I thought, would be a positive, healthy experience for them.

I purchased one half of the duplex on 39th Place for them; the other half was still occupied by Ron's family. I think the move may have added at least twenty years to my parents' lives. I was happy to be able to bring them some relief from their sadness. If nothing more, the move afforded them respite from years of back-breaking, demanding travail in the butcher shop. And I could keep a watchful eye on them if they were close to me.

My father started a small garden in his California back yard. There he planted all sorts of seeds and relaxed in the sun as he tilled the soil. One of the first fruits of his labor was a mammoth banana squash, one which was almost as large as his small self. I can still see him standing in front of his house, a huge, happy smile on his face, his eyes twinkling as he lovingly held his giant squash in both arms close to him, like a baby, or perhaps a Torah.

Settled in their home on 39th Place, Papa obtained a job as a *schochet* in a nearby chicken market. Weekends he functioned as rabbi at a little storefront synagogue walking distance from his home. He enjoyed his small garden, and Mama seemed content with her housework. They both appeared to be healing.

While married to Ron, I became pregnant several times, each time spontaneously aborting, always around the sixth week. The last of these pregnancies landed me in the hospital with a severe systemic infection. There, having time to think, I understood that my body was rejecting both the marriage and the child that might have been produced from it. This was not what I wanted. I did not like the wifely, domestic role which had been prescribed for me by my parents and society. I did not like Ron. There in the hospital I made the clear decision to leave him as soon as I was able. It was time to leave and get on with my life. My academic interest, deeply buried during the war years, sprang once again to life.

One hot day in August, 1947, I took the Red Car to Westwood, to the University of California, Los Angeles (UCLA), in search of my interrupted education. When I arrived there I was given a friendly reception by Dr. Orda Plunkett, Professor of Mycology. I described my academic background to him. He confessed his need for an assistant and promised to study my transcripts and let me know; he would be happy to consider me. My degrees, both from leading institutions, must have convinced him. In September 1947, I matriculated to UCLA for my Ph.D. in botany with a specialty in medical mycology. I was granted a teaching assistantship working with Dr. Plunkett.

I am eternally grateful to the 77th Congress of the United States, which was responsible for passing the Servicemen's Readjustment Act, the G.I. Bill, in 1944. Fortuitously it enabled me to attend graduate school for the next four years. My books, tuition, and all related academic expenses were free to me, paid for by the government. In addition, I received a monthly stipend of $50 to help with my living expenses. Frosting on the cake was the small but welcome salary I made as a teaching assistant. I knew I could stay afloat financially without being dependent upon anybody, either Ronald or my parents.

Before taking final steps toward my divorce, I felt a need to pause, to ruminate, to re-examine my life from the time I left Columbia in 1941 to this time in 1947 when I was about to return to my interrupted education. Almost seven years had elapsed. I sat down to carefully rethink my twenty-eight years of life:

I was a special kind of American, a first-generation American, the girl child of immigrant parents who, oppressed, had fled a wretched life under the Romanov tzar in Russia. From birth I had often heard terrifying stories from my mother and father about their lives in Europe. I carried in my flesh the scars of their brutal experiences. How could I do less than give all my energy, my life, if need be, to fight the burgeoning tyranny of anti-Semitism which was sweeping Europe in the '30s and '40s? I could not permit such atrocities to occur anywhere in the world, especially not here at home.

In 1919, America, the land of my birth, was a relatively new land to Jews. We had not yet established ourselves in large numbers over generations. It was clear that anti-Semitism was an acceptable way of life. I felt deeply that we Jews were in a precarious state, tentatively awaiting yet another shoe to fall. Hitler's threat to annihilate all of us was serious and palpable to me. My mind-set at age twenty-three when I entered the Navy was to resist oppression of any sort, anywhere, against my people. I was very proud of my ancient Hebrew heritage. I was weary of the suffering we Jews had been forced to bear because of our beliefs—in so many places in the world and for so many generations. Fight was in my blood. I would never flee; I would sooner die fighting. I am proud to have served in the Navy of the United States. I am proud I helped win the war against Germany.

My parents held the restrictive view that women should not be too highly educated lest men find them undesirable as wives. When, early in my life, I had declared my wish to be a medical doctor, they refused to hear such "ridiculous" talk. My brother, Solly, was to be the doctor! Although we were poor, I could expect financial help from them only to the point of obtaining a teaching credential. After that I was on my own. By war's beginning I already held this credential, and no more money would be forthcoming. Marriage and children were mandated for me, and I yielded, against my will, to the notion that I was obligated to marry and bear children. I thought I had forever lost my chance to obtain further education. But in truth I had, at war's end, gained a precious opportunity to obtain a doctorate through the G.I. Bill. I was now on a fresh new path, one I had chosen for myself, not the one that had been prescribed for me. Sadly I had lost my brother. Happily I had gained a new freedom.

I loved returning to the university. Once again at work with a microscope in a laboratory, I felt completely at ease. I loved studying and learning. Dr. Plunkett was a superb teacher, compatible with me in every respect, except for one failing—he loved women, any and all of them. Since I worked closely with him, it was difficult at times to drive him off, but I fell back on my Navy experience, where I had had to learn to manage unwanted sexual advances.

Dr. Plunkett was a natural wonder. A fat man, unattractive and unpolished, he possessed, nonetheless, a wealth of mycological knowledge. He had taken his doctorate at the University of Illinois. From his unrefined manner I surmised that he had been raised on a farm. I really knew nothing of his background. He was in his late forties when I met him.

For four years I worked side by side with this man and found him to be very receptive to my ideas and encouraging of my research. This afforded me great joy. In addition, I found I could share any problem with him, whether academic or personal. He was completely non-judgmental, always available for advice, and always supportive of me as well as of all his students. We called him Pappy, the father. And I tried to keep ours a proper father-daughter relationship. My father had never touched or caressed me, although I knew how much he loved me. But Pappy was unable to keep his hands from his female students.

He was married to Marie, a sweet woman who was de-
formed. Except for her hunchback, she was beautiful. She was
uneducated, totally disinterested in academic matters, a wonderful housekeeper, and an avid church-goer. Pappy never attended church. I'm not sure what they had in common. They
had no children. Something seemed to be awry in their relationship. Perhaps that was why Pappy found other women so
attractive.

Pappy often confided in me his sadness at the way in
which the other department members treated him; he felt
they were always looking down their sharp noses at him. Perhaps they felt he was too personal with his students. Perhaps
they wanted him to be more genteel, more professional.
Perhaps...who knows? But we graduate students loved him.
Those female students who could not tolerate his wandering
hands departed to other disciplines. I was not so naive as to
totally excuse his aberrant behavior; today it would be called
sexual harassment. But in 1947 I took his behavior in stride. I
loved my chosen field of study, and he was the only professor
of mycology in the botany department. I had no choice. And I
could control him, though it took effort.

Years later, when he was ready to retire, Dr. Plunkett
asked me to deliver his send-off speech at the faculty club,
where the department was holding a party in his honor. By
then, I was a research botanist with the Los Angeles County
Air Pollution Control District, doing my research at UCLA.

I was touched by his request. He knew that of all the
people in the botany department he could trust me to speak
well of him. And I did. I had difficulty holding back tears as I
related his devotion to his students and his science, of how
sorely such a knowledgeable, inspirational teacher would be
missed. "Here," I said, "is a professor impossible to replace, a
wonderful role model for all students aspiring to academic careers." I said not a word about his unwanted sexual advances;
I could make no excuse for that. To me, the good in him off-
set his sexual obsession. As a woman I had come to accept this

sort of behavior as normal for most men.

When, in 1965, he wrote a book entitled *The Fungus Diseases of Man*, he presented me with a copy in which he had inscribed: "To Ruth Ann Bobrov Glater, Ph.D., student and friend, in appreciation of her continued loyalty and devotion."

We were all in our late twenties in 1947, all of us veterans of World War II, returning to the university from an interrupted education. I was the only woman graduate student among the men. Most of the men were married, some few were not. I was in the process of obtaining a divorce. But none of us, including me, knew how to handle his or her sexuality. We were clumsy, awkward, and embarrassed by it.

As the lone woman graduate student in the department, I was the butt of all the men's innuendoes and smutty jokes. While I attempted to have a sense of humor and tolerance for their bawdy jocularity, I found their behavior very disturbing. The men knew me to be an avid and serious student, but that did not deter them. I tried to laugh along with them but, when I did, I understood I was laughing at myself, at my own femininity. It reminded me of stories I had heard when I was stationed in the Norfolk Navy Yard in Virginia, stories about white folk who would throw a coin to a black "boy" and expect him to jig for his money. I felt that I too was jigging to the men's tune. Their behavior may have been amusing, humorous, and even somewhat clever, but, in actuality, it was demeaning, confusing, and disruptive to me as a woman. It was completely inappropriate in any setting, especially in an academic one where truth is supposedly pursued.

During each of my four years at UCLA, come Christmastime, one of the students, Gordon Stanford, would sing as loud as he could: "Come all ye faithful. Come let us adore him. Come ye, oh come ye to be-e-e-ed." This he sang, staring at my breasts, a lewd grin on his face, while the men around him howled with glee at my discomfort.

My lab coat served as one of their prime inspirations. At

first, in keeping with my compulsive nature, I wore a neat, immaculately laundered white coat which occasioned them to exclaim: "Don't try to hide it, Ruthie. Can't be done." I knew what they meant. Since I had no way of disguising my gender, I decided to wear a dirty, unwashed, ill-fitting coat, full of acid holes, down to my ankles. Perhaps, I thought optimistically, the coat might deter them. But there was no turning them off, not even by making myself as unattractive as I knew how. And why should I, each day, have had to contend with this behavior?

One day Dr. Scott invited me to deliver a lecture to her plant anatomy class, a required course for all botany graduate students. Dr. Scott, a distinctly mannish, unmarried woman, was never the butt of male jokes. Every day this woman in her early fifties wore the same uniform: a man's short-sleeved white shirt, open at the neck, adorned with a green knit tie held in place by what appeared to be a bull-ring, a green Scottish plaid skirt down to her calves, and a pair of very sensible low-heeled walking oxfords. She had, apparently, solved the problem of her femininity by abandoning it. Perhaps she thought if she couldn't beat them, she would join them. But hers was not the choice I wished to make for myself.

I donned my defense, my long, acid-stained lab coat, and in my most serious academic manner, began to address the class on the microscopic anatomy of the *Poa annua* leaf, a typical monocotyledenous leaf. The men's eyes were constantly moving to my breasts and their lascivious grins, which were not apparent to Dr. Scott, kept me tense, riveted to my material, lest I lose my composure. It was difficult to lecture to them, certainly more difficult for me than if I had been one of them.

At noon, it was customary for us to gather around a long table in the plant physiology lab with our sack lunches. This was a fun time, a hilarious hour in which to relieve tensions after a hard morning's classes. We discussed and laughed at all manner of things: university policy, departmental edicts, veteran's rights, politics, etc. But invariably the conversation and jokes turned toward sex and me. It gave me a sense of being violated. The more uncomfortable I became, the more the men guffawed. I too needed some respite at noontime, but how to find it? I could withdraw into my own quiet lab with my test tubes and Petri dishes...and, often, in desperation, I did. Then I felt that I was not being a a good sport, even if the fun was all at my expense. How was I to be taken seriously? How was I to be equal to the men? How was I to be comfortable in the face of such excessive, inappropriate attention?

For a while I shared an office with Jerry Skopp, a fellow graduate student. He and I were assigned a room with two desks in one of the barracks buildings which still remained on campus following the war. It was across the road from P.B., the physics-biology building (later renamed Kinsey Hall), in which all of our classes were held. During the war these wooden buildings had been used to house ROTC offices and administrative war staff. Now, in order to accommodate the burgeoning postwar student population, they had been partitioned into small offices.

Jerry rarely appeared in our office. He kept a sleeping bag there and, now and then, when I would seek a quiet place to study, I might find him in his sleeping bag on the floor, snoring loudly. I would prod him awake before I could start my work and, perhaps, we would chat a bit. My only interest in him was as a fellow student. He was married, although unhappily. So he had told me.

One day he appeared in our office agitated. He told me his wife was suing for divorce and was naming me as correspondent. I was astounded. Where had such an idea come from? What had Jerry told her? I was very disturbed; this was patent nonsense. My fear quickly turned to anger. Was it not enough that I had to contend with the men's banter? Now must I also contend with their wives' jealousy? I had never even met Mrs. Skopp!

Jerry's wife soon divorced him; I heard nothing more

about the part I had unsuspectingly played in their dishar-
mony. But I had to threaten Jerry with a lawsuit should my
name be mentioned in their divorce proceedings. And why
should it have been necessary for me to face this anxiety, simply because I shared an office with another woman's husband?

I have detailed only a few of the many trials and tribula-
tions that I, as a female, encountered as I attempted to enter
the men's lair, the strictly male enclave. Many women, possibly most, would not have been able to tolerate the serious
abuse to which I was subjected. Many women might have
turned away, given up in anger and disgust.

I knew I was equal—perhaps even superior academically—to the men with whom I was studying, yet they were
treating me as an ongoing bawdy joke. I did not poke fun at
them, nor did I ever wish to. Why their unwarranted behavior
toward me? Now, many years later, I have come to understand
how difficult it is for the unenlightened male to accept a
woman into his workplace; sex always seems to get in the way.
If a man does not understand how to control his primal sexual
urge, he always has the dirty joke, the shame, the ridicule, the
"put-down" to help him in his struggle to maintain equilibrium. Our society has taught men that it is acceptable for
them to be aggressive while the woman remains passive. The
male pattern is to attack, usually through laughter, through
jive, through off-color jokes. The matter is discussed in Martin Grotjahn's book *Beyond Laughter*. "Laughter," this psychiatrist says, "occurs when libido is released from repressed
aggression." Whether or not one agrees with this Freudian interpretation, I know instinctively and from experience that
while male banter toward women may appear good natured
on the surface, it can in fact be very cruel. It wasn't until I left
the student world and entered the mature world of academia
that I realized that the clever quips of those fledgling male
students (soon to be full-grown academicians) were being
honed into sharp swords with which to cut women profession-

als down, should they wish.

In my last year in graduate school I decided to proceed
with the final steps of my divorce from Ronald. However, I
needed to first finish my doctoral exams. I collected an assort-
ment of textbooks containing the information for which I
knew I was responsible, locked myself in the spare room of
my house, and came out only long enough to fix myself a bit
of food at mealtime. There, alone and undisturbed, I studied
from early morning 'til late at night. For three weeks I read,
memorized, cogitated, questioned, and tested myself. For
three weeks I did not know or care when Ron came and went.
I had only one thing on my mind: my oral exams. After that I
would handle my failed marriage. Pappy offered to take my
classes until I returned.

My five-professor committee was to meet in the coffee
room for my oral exams, the same room where the faculty and
graduate students gathered each day at four o'clock for tea
and cookies.

It was the same room in which Dr. Epling, the taxonomy
professor, had appeared in a huff one day at tea-time and said:
"Damn it, I signed the oath of office." The University regents
had ordered that all professors and teaching and research as-
sistants were to sign a loyalty oath, an oath of allegiance to the
United States government, swearing we were not and never
had been members of the Communist Party. Not signing
meant certain dismissal. For months Dr. Epling had resisted.
So had we all. But, this day, he had capitulated. "If rape is inevitable," he said, "relax and enjoy it." Although I recognized
his words as yet another sexist remark, I agreed with his rec-
ommendation to sign. Having no recourse, we all signed.

In that same room, during afternoon break, work was put
aside for half an hour or so, and all the staff relaxed and socialized. There, also, all doctoral exams were administered at
appointed times in the mornings. After four years in the department, I felt quite at home in that room.

On the day of my doctoral exams, I paced the hall waiting for the professors of my committee to gather: Dr. Haupt, a morphologist; Dr. Plunkett, chairman of my committee and mycologist; Dr. Flora Scott, anatomist; Dr. Salle, bacteriologist; and Dr. Hammer, physiologist. I felt as if I were about to face a firing squad. Literally, my life depended upon my success. Judging from my history, where but in school had I had any success or happiness? My marriage was in shambles. Despite the men's sexual attention I could not see myself as an attractive, desirable woman. I was obviously not even able to reproduce, as could most women. This was a fight for the only thing I valued or felt secure in—my identity as a scholar.

The time had come. I stood in front of the blackboard, a long table in front of me. To the rear of the room, facing me, sat the five professors at another long table parallel to mine. There were several feet of distance—and a whole world—between us. I held a piece of chalk in my hand as the professors, one at a time, fired questions at me.

First it was Dr. Salle's turn. He asked me about the bacterial enzymes, about which I knew little. He had recently written a successful bacteriology textbook which I had read, re-read, and read again. At best, I was a poor chemistry student. The chemistry of the bacterial enzymes was of little interest to me. "Dr. Salle, if I should be in need of information on bacterial enzymes at any time, I would turn to the chapter in your book that starts on approximately page 200."

Lucky for me, and thanks to my fairly photographic memory, it was approximately the right place. The professors laughed. My tension eased a bit. There were still four professors to go.

It was now Dr. Haupt's turn. He wished to discuss with me the concept of Alternation of Generations in plants. Did I feel that the haploid stage, even if it were represented by a single cell, could be considered a generation?

"Yes," I said, "I think that even one cell can be considered a generation."

"I don't agree with you," he said testily. "One needs more than one cell to make a generation."

"Well," I shot back, "it seems like you and I are looking at the same thing from opposite sides of the fence."

"Hmm," he said, "I'm through."

Dr. Plunkett's questions were a breeze. Nobody in the room knew much about the fungi except me and him. I had been studying mycology for years, even as far back as undergraduate school. So that question-and-answer period went smoothly.

Dr. Scott asked me a few relatively easy questions regarding plant anatomy. No sweat there.

Dr. Hammer asked the last question. "In order to increase the yield of a crop in the field, what would you consider to be the most influential factor?"

I thought for a few moments, then said, "I would attempt to increase the ambient CO_2 by using huge fans hooked up to CO_2 generators. I'm not sure this would work, and I don't know if it has ever been done, but it might be worth a try."

He accepted my answer without comment, and we were through. Each professor had taken a shot at me. I was told to wait outside the door for their decision.

A few minutes later the door opened and the professors filed out, all smiles. One by one they shook my hand. I was in! I could not hold back my tears. Even as I write I feel the pride and joy of acceptance. My hopes and dreams of being an academic scientist now seemed possible.

But academia was not to treat me as well from then on. I may have been recognized by my committee as a budding, qualified Ph.D. candidate on her way to a doctorate, but I was also a woman and a Jew, factors that made all the difference in 1950.

Post-war America was in flux in the '50s. Society was attempting to soften its strong anti-Semitic prewar stance. This did not mean it was taking Jews to its heart, or that the problem of anti-Semitism had been solved, but at least things were better than they had been. On the other hand, women who, during the war, had been welcomed into the workplace, were now being told to go home. Many of them welcomed the opportunity to leave their jobs and return home, but it was the men, especially, who wanted their women back in the old time-honored domestic role. For too many years men in the military had faced death and uncertainty in foreign lands far from home. And those who had returned, who had made it through the war, wanted the stability and comfort of a family life. Rosie the Riveter was being called back to hearth and home, and the baby boom started. But there were many women who, like me, wished for something more than the domestic role.

But the day I took my oral exams in 1950, my joy knew no bounds. I had brought a sandwich from home. The male graduate students had bought a keg of beer to celebrate. We adjourned to Bob Harris' apartment near the university and whooped it up. Lots of noise, merriment, laughter, and off-color stories. Still I was the only woman present, the only non-drinker, and the butt of their off-color jokes. It was nothing new; I had become inured to it.

All that I had left to do was to finish writing and defending my dissertation. This was not difficult, just laborious. It was not an insurmountable challenge. I knew I could do it.

George Livingstone had just finished defending his dissertation in plant physiology. He was sitting at his desk in front of one of the huge windows of the plant physiology lab when I stopped to congratulate him. He had been offered a teaching position in a college up north. Much to my embarrassment, tears welled up in my eyes and slowly trickled down my cheeks. True, I was happy for him, but my tears were in anticipation of defending my own dissertation and finishing my own degree. My happiness and self-esteem depended so much upon the scientific community's acceptance of my scholastic ability. I had been working toward this goal all my life. Now I was almost home.

Before I defended my dissertation, I knew that one thing remained to be done: I finally needed to finish unburdening myself of Ronald. He was still fumbling along, unable to make a living.

I must admit that I went about dissociating myself from him in a bizarre and cowardly way. Not having the courage to face him squarely and tell him that I no longer wished to be his wife, I swiftly and without warning moved out of our house, lock, stock, and barrel. This was on a Saturday just after he had gone to his office. There was no negotiating. No therapy. No goodbyes. I did it this way despite my better, more humane instincts. It seemed easier that way at that moment.

The following Monday I consulted an attorney and filed papers for divorce. Ronald did not contest it. I then moved in with my parents, paid them for room and board, and continued my work at the university. My parents seemed content to have me home again, although I was rarely there except on weekends. Usually I spent my only day off, Sunday, working in the garden, washing my car, doing my laundry, and relaxing. In the late-afternoon I would retire to the quiet of my room, turn on my little radio and listen to the late afternoon comedians, Jack Benny, Fibber McGee and Molly, Edgar Bergen, and Phil Harris and Alice Faye. After a day away from the university, refreshed, I was ready to return to my lab on Monday. I did not give my failed marriage much thought.

For the next year or so I lived with my parents. They were a peaceful couple. Although my mother continued to dominate my father as she always had, he appeared to live comfortably under her yoke. He still had his garden and little synagogue, and these seemed enough to satisfy him.

I spent long days at the university doing my research, digging in the literature. There were Portuguese, Spanish, German, and French scientific papers to pore over. The French and German papers I could handle on my own. When I needed help with the other languages, I was able, for a little money, to find a language student to assist me. Finally, having plowed through all the pertinent American and foreign literature I could find, I was convinced that I had done a thorough job of gathering all that was known about the genus *Geotrichum.*

The genus *Geotrichum* (all seventeen strains of it) was the topic of my dissertation. *Geotrichum* was a simple fungus, one of the fungi imperfecti. No sexual stage had ever been reported for it, nor was I ever able to induce one, try as I might. Often, when transferring from a mother colony to fresh sterile agar plates, two or three colonies would appear, colonies which differed both from the mother colony and from one another in morphology and biochemistry. This puzzled me. After long thought, I came to the conclusion that the numerous nuclei present in a single mycelium were probably different from one another. This meant that a single mycelial strand might actually be a colony of different nuclei, rather than a collection of like nuclei. In conclusion, I was able to describe seventeen strains, all differing from one another, all having arisen from a single mycelial strand. There was no need to assign them distinct species names because, should I continue to transfer, colonies might appear which were yet different from the seventeen I had already described. Or could it be that this organism was constantly mutating?

Dr. Plunkett promised to have my dissertation, "A Study of the Genus *Geotrichum*," published by the University of California Press, but by the time he got around to submitting my monograph, it was too late. He had waited too long. "If it had been submitted sooner…," the University of California Press said. However, the dissertation was complete, signed, and sealed. I delivered it to Powell Library to be bound and placed in the library stacks for reference and perpetuity. The matter of its publication was not as important to Dr. Plunkett as it was to me.

I was divorced—a free woman. I was approaching thirty and had already done a heap of living. In early 1951, I de-

fended my dissertation. I suppose I knew more about the genus *Geotrichum* than anybody else in the world. My committee members were experts in their fields; I knew mine. And I
was secure in that knowledge.

The day I defended my dissertation was one of the happiest days of my life. It may have been the happiest. I knew that
I had at least been exposed to all aspects of botanical and mycological knowledge to that point in time. I knew that I was a
fledgling doctor of philosophy, a bona fide scientist, a botanist
with a specialty in mycology and more especially in medical
mycology. I respected myself for having spent the last four
difficult, demanding years studying, reviewing, and honing my
skills. In all, I had spent ten years in universities. I felt satisfied with my training, and, finally, I felt deserving of the degree I was about to receive.

Graduation day, the 14th of June 1951, was the culmina-
tion of my formal years of university study. Both my mother
and father proudly attended my graduation, which was held at
the Hollywood Bowl. When I donned my cap and gown, Dr.
Scott, in cap and gown herself, preparing to march in the faculty procession, arranged my blue-and-gold cowl, the colors of
the University of California. "Another Ph.D. woman scientist,"
she said proudly as she placed the cap with the gold tassel on
my head. My doctoral gown had the three traditional black
velvet bands on the sleeve. I had never before or since felt so
fulfilled.

But I was truly worried. I had applied to university after
university for a teaching post in botany and/or mycology and
had received nothing but rejections. Dr. Hammer, chairman
of the botany department, had written a strong letter of rec-
ommendation on my behalf. Isolde, the secretary of the department, told me so. Dr. Hammer had stated that I was one
of the finest Ph.D. candidates his department had ever produced. In spite of his letter and others of equal praise from
other members of my committee, only one university bit; the
University of Idaho at Moscow. I was ready to go anywhere in

or out of the U.S.—even to Moscow, Russia, if it meant a university position.

I met with the chairman of the botany department of the University of Idaho in the lobby of the Biltmore hotel in Los Angeles. He appeared impressed with my credentials. And then he dropped a bomb. "What is your religion?" he said. "I am a Jew," I answered. If that information registered, he did not show it. Then he said, "I would hire you on the spot if you were a man, but the members of my department would be furious if I were to bring a woman into the department." But certainly he had known I was a woman when he initially invited me to meet with him! Aside from Babe Ruth, are there any other men with the given name Ruth? Could it be that I wasn't attractive enough? Or was I too attractive? Was it the sex issue? Did it have to do with my religion?

Today in compliance with Title VII of the Civil Rights Act (1964), no university spokesperson would dare to ask (let alone bar) a candidate for his or her race, color, religion, national origin, sex, or even sexual preference. But in 1950 many people spoke bigotry and prejudice openly. Occasionally, one might detect a tinge of apology for this, but no bona fide shame. Whatever the cause, I knew myself to be an excellent teacher and a qualified researcher. He could not have disqualified me on the basis of my academic record. On which count had he barred me?

Still undaunted, I took the train to Tucson, Arizona, hoping against hope that the University of Arizona might be in need of a mycologist. There were not many of us around.

The last time I had visited Tucson was in 1944, during the war, while still in uniform. On a few days' leave from the Navy, I had visited the University of Arizona; universities always attracted me. The huge saguaro cacti (*Carnegiea gigantea*) were being infected by a fungus or bacterium which threatened to destroy the magnificent forests of the lower Arizona deserts. The chairman of the botany department had asked me if I would consider leaving the military to work on this problem. I explained I could not accept a position until the war was over.

Now the war was over, and I had completed my doctorate. Possibly the University of Arizona could use my services. I took a room at a hotel and, early the next morning, arrived at the university, uninvited, unannounced. The chairman of the botany department, whom I had met during the war, had by now been replaced by a younger man. He was not interested. "We already have one woman professor in the department. I cannot hire another." I had deliberately not written to Arizona beforehand because I thought if I were seen in person, I might not be so easily dismissed. But here was yet another crushing rejection. And after such an expensive trip! It was my fault; the university hadn't invited me to come. I had only myself to blame.

Following graduation, all of my fellow male students easily acquired academic positions. But I could not. What was I to do? Become a masculine woman? Cut my hair short like a man, stride, talk in a deep voice, bind my breasts, swear celibacy, take an oath never to bear children? I grew angrier and more despondent as I realized the naked, unvarnished truth; male Ph.D. scientists were being hired upon graduation, their contracts signed even before they held a diploma in their hands. I, a female, was not even given an interview. There was no question that I was being discriminated against. Tim Harwood had immediately been hired by the University of Mississippi at Biloxi, Harris Greene by the University of Arizona (where only a few months earlier I had been rejected), Jerry Skopp by the University of California at Davis—and he didn't even want the job; it was offered to him! Instead, Skopp emigrated to Australia to be a sheep rancher. With each new rejection my initial euphoria at having attained my doctorate grew dimmer.

In my last semester at UCLA, I had taken a seminar with Dr. Scott. She and I met once a week to discuss research done by leading researchers in plant anatomy. One day I was reviewing a chapter on hydrophytes, plants growing in rivers and streams. I was quoting from a text I had read. Dr. Scott took issue with a statement I made.

"Where did you get that information?" she asked testily.

"I got it from Dr. Miller's book," I said.

"Well, don't believe everything you read," she said. "You are beyond the textbook. You'll soon be writing your own."

High praise. Fine encouragement. Thank you, Dr. Scott. But I could not even get a job, let alone write a book.

Desperate, my thoughts turned to civil service. Certainly the United States government would not be prejudiced against women. I applied for a botanist's position with the Atomic Energy Commission, which had an office on campus at UCLA and completed a long, complicated application. Among the multitude of questions was the one which, I believe, did me in: What was your mother's and father's birthplace? "Russia," I wrote. I believe that to have been the death knell for my non-career with the AEC.

My parents had come to this country in 1904 when they were teenagers. They very soon became naturalized citizens. They were loyal Americans. They hated Russia with a passion. So strong was their hatred for the country of their birth that from the moment they set foot in America, they spoke no Russian, only Yiddish. As for me, I had been cleared to handle top-secret documents while still a civilian supervisory clerk in the War Department in 1940. In addition, for almost three years during the war, I had served as an officer in the U.S. Navy, where I handled secret troop movements. Yet was I not a loyal enough American to hold a job with the AEC? Was it because my parents had been born in Russia?

The job went instead to Barbara James, a master's graduate student of very limited academic ability. Why did she get the job and not I? Possibly it was Senator Joe McCarthy, the super-patriotic American, who had decided my fate. Dagger held high, he righteously claimed the power to stab and kill. Right and left, mostly left, he attempted to destroy anybody who had even the remotest connection with anything Russian. My parents had made the grave mistake of having been born in Russia.

I thought to leave the country, perhaps for Israel. I had joined the Navy and delayed my education in order to help protect my people. Perhaps it was time now to join them in Israel. The Americans obviously didn't want me.

It was 1950. The state of Israel had only been in existence for two years, having been established in 1948. It was a struggling young country in much turmoil. Before it could get its act together, almost from the day of its birth, it was at war with the Arabs. This did not deter me. Trying to find an Israeli in Los Angeles who could direct me how to emigrate proved impossible, though I learned, much later, much too late, that a man named Rubin Datni had been appointed Israeli consul in Los Angeles as early as 1948. If he (or any other Israeli with whom I could speak) had been there, I could not find him or her, much as I tried.

In a scientific journal, I discovered the name of an Israeli Ph.D., a woman doing mycological research at the Weizman Institute in Rehoveth. I sent her my resume and transcripts. She wrote back promptly to tell me they would be delighted to have me but had no money to help with my transportation. If I were to pay my own way, they would consider hiring me. That put me in an impossible situation. I had no money to go to Israel on the mere possibility of a job. That was a long way to travel without a commitment. Besides, I did not know Hebrew well enough to function, although she assured me I would be given intensive Hebrew language training at no cost.

Today Israel, firmly established after more than forty-five years, is happy to have young American scientists emigrate, male or female. The office of Aliyah at the Jewish Federation in Los Angeles, has the major function of recruiting professionals for work in Israel and expedites all the myriad details involved in such a move. But in 1950, with nobody to whom to turn, I felt that even my own people were excluding me.

Under the Glass Ceiling

The diploma which I had received from UCLA stated that because of my ability in original research I was granted the degree of doctor of philosophy in botany and, in bold letters, added "with all the rights and privileges thereto pertaining." As I worked at my laboratory bench cleaning my flasks and Petri dishes, preparing to leave the university for good, I pondered what those rights and privileges might be to me, a woman and a Jew. Suddenly, a voice broke into my sad thoughts. "Hey, Ruth, I think I've found a job for you."

It was Milt Zaitlin, a beginning graduate student in plant physiology. He had just returned from an American Association for the Advancement of Science (AAAS) meeting in Pasadena, where he had run into an old friend, Bill Noble.

Bill was a former high school chemistry teacher who was now working for the Los Angeles County Air Pollution Control District (APCD). The crops in and around Los Angeles were mysteriously being damaged before they could be brought to market. The cause of the damage was yet unknown.

Bill loved plants. Since there was no botanist on staff, the APCD, in its wisdom, sent the plant-loving chemist into the fields to assess crop damage and to talk with and perhaps to soothe the distraught farmers as best he could. Aside from his interest in plants, Bill knew little botany. He needed the help of a trained botanist, somebody who could talk knowledgeably with the growers and help discover why their plants were dying. Milt told Bill about me and Bill asked that I call him. I did, immediately.

The offices of the APCD were on Santa Fe Street in downtown Los Angeles, surrounded on all sides by heavy industry. Finding my way there was difficult. I had never before been in industrial Los Angeles, and I was a new driver to boot. Traffic was congested. Large, cumbersome, clattering trucks moved in every direction. The stench from the Bandini manure processing plant down the street was unbearable. Tears streamed down my face from the foul air. This, I thought, is a most appropriate place for an air pollution office. I made my way, nervously, into the building.

Bill Noble, a small man with graying hair, was very pleasant. When he got up to greet me, I observed that he was crippled. He had had polio as a child and was left seriously impaired. However, he managed to get around quite well hobbling. I had brought my resume with me. He skimmed it, seemingly pleased, and then explained what he would need of me. I was to travel the fields of L.A. County observing the effects the polluted air was having on the crops of farmers and nurserymen. I would be responsible for policing the entire eighty-mile radius of the county. "I will sometimes accompany you," he said, "but most often you'll have to go it alone. I'll go with you until you become familiar with the territory."

There was no job description on the county civil service roster for a botanist; the closest listing was photomicroscopist. If I was interested, he would use that slot to hire me. Later he would see to it that a research botanist slot be created. He apologized for the salary, $337 a month, approximately what the clerks were earning. He was sure the Civil Service Commission would soon upgrade the salary.

"Are you interested?" he said. Then he pleaded, "Please be interested!"

I said yes on the spot. This job was certainly not what I wanted, not job-wise and absolutely not salary-wise. It was an inspector's job. Perhaps at some future date I might be able to mold it into applied research. It had become quite clear to me that I had better take whatever job I was offered; academia was obviously not going to make room for me. I had seriously searched for months without success.

I went to work for the APCD in early July, 1951. On my very first day at work I was approached by a blond, blue-eyed young man, a chemist in the large lab which dominated the first floor of the building. Bud Glater was talkative, anxious to show me around. I had no office; my time at first was to be spent inspecting crops in the field, and having no office made little difference to me. Meanwhile, on those occasions when I visited the downtown headquarters, I would invariably run into Bud. He would drop whatever he was doing to chat with me; his unrequested attention embarrassed me.

My new job entailed lots of traveling. I had just barely learned to drive my Studebaker, and it was totally undependable. I later learned, much to my chagrin, that this supposedly new car had been in a flood somewhere in the country. The crook who sold it to me had deliberately failed to tell me this. The car was more in the shop than on the road. And then one day a mechanic at the Studebaker agency accidentally divulged the truth. As the result of a flood, he admitted, the caked, dry mud in the motor kept jamming things up. However, this knowledge did me little good. I did not have the money or the stomach to sue the car dealer. Besides, it fit a pattern I was becoming accustomed to: a male had, once again, recognized that he could put one over on an unsuspecting female. I'm sure he would never have dared to unload this lemon on a man!

Luckily, the county gave me a dependable government car to drive on my field trips. However, with very little sense of direction, I was nervous as I drove through the lonely countryside alone. I had always had difficulty finding my way to new places, and I hated maps, on which I was now forced to depend. I knew my way around a laboratory, but not around the open fields of Los Angeles County. I kept thinking, this job is for an inspector type who has had one or more high school botany courses and loves to drive. Hardly a job for an academic scientist. Yet I needed a job; no other was available to me.

Bill was aware of my apprehension about driving alone. At first, sensing my discomfort, he accompanied me to the outlying farm areas, introducing me to the many farmers and growers along the way. He had discovered, in the course of his trips, that the crops and ornamental plants in all of Los Angeles County were being damaged to the point of being unsalable. But he did not know how or why this was happening, although some type of air pollution was suspected.

Those growers who were in the city or within easy reach of it were no problem for me. Armacost and Royston, the orchid grower, was located in West Los Angeles. No problem there. The Kentia palm grower was in Palms, a section of West Los Angeles, close in. Easy. It was the distant places in the county that threw me into panic—Puente, Fullerton, Rosemead, Burbank, Pomona, Pasadena, and beyond. While I really enjoyed meeting and discussing problems with the growers (plant people are mostly a congenial lot), driving alone through deserted roads was not my cup of tea, especially as night began to fall.

After a few months of inspecting fields and greenhouses, I knew I would soon need to revamp my job to better suit my training and personality. In my travels it had become clear to me that most agricultural crops could not survive the polluted air of L.A. I knew I would ultimately need a laboratory and a microscope. But first I wanted to observe research in progress at the California Institute of Technology (Cal Tech). For the next several months I worked there with Drs. Fritz Went and Herb Hull and came to realize that I needed to know more about what was occurring inside the plant where no botanist had yet looked. With the unaided eye, one could easily observe gross damage markings, but what was happening inside the leaf itself? Soon a small lab was set up for me in the APCD headquarters on Santa Fe Street. I rolled up my sleeves and started my research. In a laboratory with a microscope I felt capable of attacking the problem.

Working at the main office on Santa Fe Street, I had the opportunity to interact with the staff chemists, meteorologists, and engineers. From them I learned about the chemistry and meteorology of the atmosphere and what techniques were being used to better understand the specific chemistry of the Los Angeles air. I learned that refined gasoline vapors were combining with ozone in the air to produce ozonated hydrocarbons and peroxyacetyl nitrate, reaction products which were often held close to the ground by an inversion layer that moved up and down each day as atmospheric conditions changed. These reaction products, I soon determined, were harmful to plants and probably to people and animals as well—especially on days when the inversion layer hugged the ground.

As my work progressed, I described how these noxious, airborne gases entered the plants through the stomata in their leaves. The growing points, the apical meristems, seemed to survive, and the plants continued to grow, though marginally. However, the mature leaves and flowers of most crops were so severely damaged they could not be brought to market. These included spinach, orchid blossoms, ferns, and most other leafy crops. Vegetables of all sorts were becoming unmarketable, presenting a serious economic loss to the agricultural community of Southern California.

On smoggy days I would often step outside the back door of the building on Santa Fe Street for a brief respite from my work. After several hours at the microscope, the polluted air (which had been superheated by my microscope's lamp) caused tears to stream down my face and my nasal tissues to swell. Breathing became difficult. One such day a police car drove into our parking lot and stopped in front of me. Two burly cops got out.

"What are you going to do about this air?" one said to me, tears running down his cheek. "I can't even see to drive!"

"Join the club," I answered. In a few words I attempted to explain what was happening to the once-balmy, refreshing, breathable air of Los Angeles. And that we had no immediate solution.

Air pollution research was pointing an accusing finger at the automobile and petroleum industries, which were pouring refined gasoline vapor into the atmosphere without restraint. It became apparent that it was necessary to reduce (or at least to limit) the number of private automobiles being driven in L.A. county on a daily basis. Mass transportation might be a likely solution, or at least a palliative. But nobody cared to hear the suggestions of those of us doing research at the APCD.

As more and more people continued to pour into the L.A. basin from other parts of the country, each family adding one, two, or more cars to the already massive number, the APCD's attempt to limit gasoline emissions proved futile. Neither the public nor the petroleum industry nor the automobile industry cared to heed our recommendations. More than forty years later, Los Angeles, still gasping for fresh air, its agricultural capacity seriously compromised, is attempting an electric mass transportation system and a subway. But Los Angelenos, I fear, have too passionate a love affair with their automobiles to ever abandon them in favor of public transportation, even should it become available.

Soon after my lab was established, I published the first description of the damage that occurred to the interior anatomy of susceptible leaves. The many spinach farmers in southwest Los Angeles and those scattered amongst the gasoline storage tanks of Torrance and El Segundo, unable to bring their crops to market, cashed out and sold their fields to rapacious real estate developers. Once a flourishing agricultural county, Los Angeles seemed able to grow only new houses on its land, not edible crops.

My work at the APCD began to heat up. A paper I wrote, entitled "The Leaf Structure of *Poa annua* with Observations on its Smog Sensitivity in Los Angeles County," appeared in

May 1955 in the *American Journal of Botany*. It was the first description of how smog damaged the interior tissues of leaves. The pen-and-ink diagram of a *Poa annua* leaf, which I drew to illustrate the paper, was eight feet long by two feet wide. After its publication and with the APCD's permission, I donated the drawing to the Plant Anatomy Lab at UCLA. Because of its size and clarity, Dr. Scott hung it in her classroom, where her students could easily see and study the anatomy of a typical monocotyledonous leaf.

Soon scientists came to my lab to observe my techniques of staining and sectioning leaf tissue by hand without the use of a microtome. Using a microtome demanded the tissue be frozen; this, I felt, might alter the cells in some subtle ways. So I worked only with fresh leaves, sectioning them using a hand-held razor blade. It required only a steady hand and a sharp cutting edge. Sometimes I used pith in which to embed the fresh tissue; more often I rolled the tissue upon itself to form a rigid tube which I could then slice easily.

While the work was new and stimulating, it was not what I had been trained for, nor was it what I wanted. My title had soon been changed to research botanist but my salary remained minuscule. Money aside, I still yearned for a tenure-track professorship in botany or mycology. Whichever way I attempted to explain to myself my inability to obtain such a position, it made no sense. With each new acknowledgment by my peers of my ability as a scientist, I agonized over why no university offered me a post. I had made it clear to everyone that that was what I wanted.

As time wore on I began, little by little, to turn against myself, questioning my ability. I was aware of an insidious depression settling in. I continued to measure myself against the successful male professors who spoke glowingly of Bobrov's "elegant research." They were not more knowledgeable or capable than I. Why was I being passed over? Something, I thought, must be very wrong with me.

Insight into these questions came years later, as I was

writing this book. Dr. Jane De Hart, professor of history at
the University of California at Santa Barbara, knowing of my
frustration, presented me with a copy of Jonathan Cole's book,
Fair Science: Women in the Scientific Community, a book I
read with avid interest. The author clearly explains the negative feelings most women scientists experienced toward themselves during those early days of the 1950s.

Women scientists, Dr. Cole stated, have historically (prior
to 1960) faced three prominent barriers to becoming fully
productive members of the scientific community. He refers to
this as "the triple penalty":

"*First*, science is culturally defined as an inappropriate career for women; the number of women recruited to science is
thereby reduced below the level which would obtain were this
definition not prevalent. *Second*, those women who have sur-
mounted the first barrier and have become scientists, continue to be hampered by the belief that women are less competent than men. Whatever the validity of this belief, it con-
tributes to women's ambivalence towards their work and
thereby reduces their motivation and commitment to scientific careers. And *third*...there is some evidence for actual
discrimination against women in the scientific community. To
the extent that women scientists suffer from these disadvan-
tages, they are victims of one or more components of the
triple penalty."

Great sorrow overcame me as I realized that my failure to
achieve academic parity with men was not solely my fault;
mine was a struggle against an insurmountable tide. I identified completely with Dr. Cole's analysis of the predicaments of
women in science.

First, "science is...an inappropriate career for women." I
had to fight hard to overcome the cultural barrier to my entering the field of science. My traditional, conservative parents
were opposed to my choice of an academic career. So were all
of my relatives and friends. And, most of all, society was op-

posed. By no one was I encouraged in my struggle.

Second, there is the notion that "women are less competent than men," meaning that women are not as creative, not
as wise, and not as well-qualified physiologically, psychologi-
cally, or emotionally as men. Hence my brother (who did not
have the grades to enter medical school) was not only expected but in fact ordered to attend dental school at great expense to my parents, whereas I was limited to studying for a
teaching credential if I wished any university training at all.

Third, "there is...actual discrimination against women in
the scientific community." When I finally graduated after ten
difficult years of graduate school, having received high praise
from my professors for my scholastic ability, I faced real discrimination in job opportunities. Witness that all the men who
attended graduate school with me were hired by universities
even before their graduation.

Not only was the triple penalty exacted of me because of
my gender, my religion was an added stone. I was a Jew in a
day when campuses were not opened to Jews. Quotas for
Jewish-American graduate students were openly defended by
presidents of leading universities, including Nicholas Murray
Butler, president of Columbia University. I have just dusted
off my master's diploma from this prestigious institution; it is
indeed signed by the same Nicholas Murray Butler, a signa-
ture faded with age, dated 1941. Much to my chagrin, I was
an unwanted guest at Columbia! Positions on university and
college faculties were also closed to Jewish-American professors until some years after WWII.

As a woman scientist in the '50s, I found myself between a
rock and a hard place, accepted neither by men nor by most
women. On the one hand, men resisted women's encroach-
ment into their space, and on the other, domestic women
(who desired to marry and stay at home) resented their liberated sisters. Betty Friedan said it well in 1963 in her famous
book *The Feminine Mystique*: A woman's success was not
measured by her own worth, but by her husband's achieve-

ments. A hostile climate hit me when I emerged from the protective cocoon of graduate school to attempt to become a professional scientist.

However, before I attained this understanding, my self-doubt was slowly but seriously eroding my health. I was working at the county APCD and living in my parents' home on La Salle Street. As the months wore on, I began to feel physically ill at work. Often the room would begin to spin and my pulse to race—80, 90, 100 and more beats per minute. In panic, I wished to rush home to bed. I was sure that the heart condition the Navy had diagnosed in 1944 was worsening. I'd best seek medical help, I thought.

A doctor at the Veterans Administration assured me that my heart was not in danger. "Your symptoms are not due to heart disease," he said. "They are due to anxiety. You need psychiatric help." Without questioning him or seeking a second opinion, I began treatment with a young psychiatrist, Dr. Milton Winter, whose office was on the eleventh floor of a downtown skyscraper on Broadway, a short distance from my Santa Fe Street lab. I saw him once a week after work. Since he was on V.A. payroll, treatment was afforded me without charge. Could all of my physical symptoms indeed be due to anxiety, I wondered? And, if so, what could be done about it?

Soon I was having therapy more than once a week. Dr. Winter was a novice, an inexperienced Freudian psychiatrist. We commenced psychoanalysis, the popular treatment of the day. I was not responding; my symptoms were not abating. If anything, I grew more anxious and suffered even more palpitations and vertigo than before. My incomprehensible fear at work intensified. Following each session with this doctor, I felt worse. The sicker I felt, the more sessions I requested and the more he provided. Cost was not a deterrent; the V.A. was paying the bill. The young chemist I had met on my first day at the APCD, Bud, and I had become friends. He would encourage me, saying "It's normal to feel worse before you feel better." But I soon felt that I was becoming addicted to the therapy, dependent upon the psychiatrist for whatever meager stability I had. My health was definitely not improving. I still carried on my job at the APCD, but without enthusiasm or interest. I was neither happy nor excited by my work.

This was the early 1950s, the heyday of psychoanalysis. Freudian therapy was considered capable of curing anything from ingrown toenails to maniacal psychosis. Lie on the couch. Talk to the air. Vent your rage and fear to the faceless person sitting behind you and with whom you dare not make eye contact. Absolute silence and incognito on the doctor's part was how it worked. And he spoke directly to you only to say, "Time's up. See you next week." He was a *tabula rasa,* an erased blackboard. No overt interaction dared occur between patient and doctor. Was this truly a way to get well?

Three years went by and I was still visiting Dr. Winter several times a week. Meanwhile he had left the V.A. and had graduated to a posh office and a private practice on Rodeo Drive in Beverly Hills. I was still plodding along as his pa-tient, but now I had to pay for his services out of pocket. The good doctor assured me that twenty dollars a session was a bargain, considering most analysts were charging at least twice that. After investing so many years, I felt I had no choice but to continue seeing him; in fact, I was hooked. My need for him was identical to that of a drug addict for a fix.

Why was I not getting better? Why did Dr. Winter never discuss with me my anger when I saw men less qualified than I being given jobs I felt I deserved? Why was this central, confounding issue in my life not being honored? Why was there no discussion of my failed wartime marriage to Ronald? Why was it becoming progressively harder for me to leave the therapist's cocoon to get on with my life? Why did we never discuss my relationship with Bud, the new man in my life? Why was conjoint therapy never suggested? Why was the vital matter of my rapidly ebbing self-esteem never discussed? Dr. Winter was not providing me with therapy. Was not "therapy" a word for healing? I was certainly not being empowered to enter the world I felt had rejected me. I lost more and more time in sick leave. I was wandering aimlessly down a path to nowhere.

Meanwhile Bud and I had grown close. Only in hindsight do I understand why I took Bud's sexual advances seriously so soon after we met, why I permitted the relationship to grow, why I glommed onto him. It is not that I found him particularly attractive, or intelligent, or interesting, or successful. It was because I saw him as a safe haven from all the confusion I had felt in the Navy, from all the sexual banter at the university, from the need to make sense of my hasty, wartime marriage in 1944, from my inability to achieve my academic goal, and from the subordinate, inappropriate job I now held which did little to fulfill me. And I was overcome with a sense of failure, both as a scientist and as a woman. I needed a devoted champion and protector. I saw Bud as that. Nearsightedly I saw him as accepting, dependable, stable, and supportive. Despite my previous failed marriage, I thought perhaps marriage to *this* man might provide the equilibrium I needed. I was acting out of confusion.

Bud and I were married at my parents' home late in the afternoon on Friday, December 31, 1953, just before the Sabbath and New Year's Eve. I called Rabbi de Koven, a Conservative rabbi, a gentle, uninspired man, to perform the Hebrew service.

The wedding was performed under a hastily erected temporary *chuppah* which the rabbi had brought with him. Standing under the wedding canopy, I wished I were a thousand miles away. I wished the wedding were over. My new husband, his family, his friends, and all those present at the ceremony were of little interest to me. I understood that my thoughts were inappropriate at such a supposedly holy time. This was a charade. What was I doing here? If I could only lie down on a bed far away from this place, alone, in peace, to think, to weep, to escape, to understand my way.

And so I had done it again! I was married for a second time. Dr. Winter offered me no advice, made no judgment, said no word, and made no attempt to discuss my sexual problems with me.

The next twenty-three years of marriage were an ongoing nightmare. At times my life was a little less tumultuous than at others, but at no time was it peaceful or serene. Bud's interaction with me was fraught with tension, more so each day. I was more unhappy in this marriage than I had been in the first. And I was similarly miserable in my professional life.

The time between the day of my wedding and the day of my divorce in March, 1977, was a vast hiatus in my life. During that time I continued to spiral downward, slowly at first, and then more and more rapidly. I was not aware of the world outside my own misery. I knew only my intense struggle to stay afloat, to keep my research job, such as it was, and to keep my husband, such as he was. Each day married to Bud was a grinding chore. I was torn between a life of domesticity and my desire for professional identity. Each day I grew more fearful. More and more I suffered tachycardia, vertigo, weakness, deepening depression, and dependency. Dr. Winter was no help; his sessions gave me only momentary relief.

At the end of 1954, Gordon Larsen left as director of the APCD to seek less hostile, greener pastures. A few days before he left he advised me to request a research grant from the United States Public Health Service. He put me in touch with people in Washington who could be of help. I therefore was successful in obtaining funding. The money was allotted to the UCLA School of Engineering. The contract stipulated that I was to be appointed research botanist in charge of a project I had proposed, entitled "A Plant Bio-assay Method for Identifying the Chemical Components of Smog." It also stipulated that I was to be provided a laboratory on campus. My position carried no university tenure and no retirement benefits. It was certainly not the professorship for which I yearned; but at least and at best it was an entree into the university system. I accepted the job knowing it to be insecure. If money was forthcoming I worked; if not, I could be dropped easily and without notice. Starting in early 1955, I began my work in the School of Engineering at UCLA. Only I and the administration knew how tenuous my situation was.

Soon after I became university staff, invitations to lecture at various research institutes and universities began to appear. Dr. Abe Zarem of the American Petroleum Institute invited me to be the guest speaker at a luncheon sponsored by his organization at the Huntington Hartford Hotel in Pasadena. Honored by the recognition, I bought a new dress befitting the occasion, a black wool dress with a tight-fitting bodice and a jaunty red hat to accompany it. I was very excited, especially when I discovered that, as the guest speaker, I was the only woman in a room of approximately two hundred men, all well-heeled engineers from prestigious companies.

Abe was very personable, jovial, and cordial. He seated me at the head table close by him and called the meeting to order. "Gentlemen," he said, "gentlemen," and then glancing over at me he hesitantly added, "uh, and ladies, uh, I mean, Dr. Bobrov." In a strong, self-assured voice I responded, "It's okay, Abe. I was a lieutenant in the WAVES and that makes me an officer and gentleman by act of Congress." Laughter went up in the room. After the luncheon, I delivered my paper, "The Effect of Smog on the Plants of Los Angeles County." While it pointed an accusing finger at the petroleum industry, nobody present seemed to take offense. The paper was graciously received, the applause generous. I must admit to being somewhat uncomfortable as the only woman in a room full of men. But, to be truthful, on some level I enjoyed the attention.

For a short time after my marriage I continued to use my maiden name when publishing or lecturing. But that ended abruptly just after I delivered a paper I was invited to give at the University of California at Riverside. Although happy to have been invited, I still smarted from the fact that I was not university faculty like the professors who had extended me the invitation.

Since I did not know my way on the freeways, I asked Bud if he would accompany me to Riverside.

"Sure," he said impatiently, "I'll take you. But why the hell can't you learn to drive on a freeway yourself?"

Here, I thought silently, angrily, is a sullen cow who gives milk then kicks over the pail. Bud knew how to hurt. Did he not see I was losing my confidence, even to drive any distance from home?

Bud was in the lecture hall the day Dr. Middleton introduced me: "Dr. Bobrov is research botanist with the School of Engineering at UCLA. She has done some elegant research on the response of plants to toxic agents in the atmosphere. And, by the way, her husband is here with her today. Would you please stand up, Mr. Bobrov?" I saw Bud flush. My name instead of his! I knew I would hear about this.

After that I began to use my married name in my professional work. But, in truth, I saw this as a further step down. At that time, I still labored under the delusion that my career and my name were secondary to those of my husband. Wasn't that the way everybody wanted it?

On another occasion, Stanford Research Institute invited me (among other scientists) to give a paper on my latest research. The paper was entitled "The Response of the Beet Leaf (*Beta vulgaris*) to Smog." Again we met at the Huntington Hartford Hotel.

I was standing on the left side of the podium absorbed in my delivery and speaking into a hand-held microphone. The few note cards which I used to guide me were on the lectern before me. It was getting close to lunchtime, and I sensed that the men (again I had a strictly male audience) were getting restless. Inadvertently, I dropped one of my cards. As I bent to retrieve it, a man gallantly jumped forward, picked it up, and handed it back to me. "Thank you," I said, forgetting the microphone still in my hand. The audience, hearing "Thank you," assumed I was through, applauded politely and began to file out of the lecture hall to a waiting lunch. But I had not yet made my point, that smog might be damaging to humans as well as plants. And so, unable to stop the exodus, I said, "Oh well, it doesn't matter. You can read the rest of my lecture in the proceedings." (All the papers which were delivered that day were to be published in a book entitled, *The Proceedings of the Stanford Research Institute*.) The next day, Matt Weinstock, a columnist for the *Los Angeles Times*, featured this amusing incident as the lead item in his daily column.

So there were some few rewarding and even fun times that punctuated my lagging professional life. I continued to do my research, and my papers continued to be published in respectable scientific journals. And invitations to speak continued to be extended to me. But I worked with increasing tension and with lessening enthusiasm, sinking deeper and deeper into melancholy. Bud never understood why I was distressed. Dr. Winter continued to see me week after week, understanding nothing, lending no helping hand.

One of the advantages of being university staff was that I was given a part-time assistant. Louis Hernandez was a young no-nonsense student working toward a master's degree in chemistry.

In 1972 the problem of lead contamination in vegetation was brought to my attention by the California State Department of Health. Fifty-four horses had died in Benicia, California, near San Francisco, from the ingestion of the tops of contaminated wild oats. The plants were reported to contain 36,000 parts per million of lead.

I knew that children had died of lead ingestion at much lower concentrations than that which had killed the horses, lead they had swallowed when eating pica, peelings of old paint which contained lead. I knew also that adults suffer in subclinical ways (nervousness, fatigue, and vague symptoms of ill health) from very low atmospheric levels of this metal.

Tetraethyl lead had been introduced into gasoline as an anti-knock additive about forty-eight years before, and lead levels were known to be increasing in the environment of large cities throughout the world. The Los Angeles basin registered even higher concentrations than those of average contaminated cities in America and abroad.

I reasoned that lead was undoubtedly being absorbed by the leaves and roots of plants growing in heavily industrialized areas and that people were ingesting the contaminated tissue. Lettuce plants seemed a good subject to study; almost everybody ate salad, and lettuce was still being cultivated abundantly in farms and fields adjacent to Los Angeles County's busy freeways. Louis and I started our lead studies with lettuce leaves and roots which we collected from a farm adjacent to the freeway in Downey, California.

At the time, atomic absorption (AA) was the only tried-and-true method for detecting lead in tissue. But that was too tedious and time-consuming for me. I wanted a histochemical method which could be used easily, would yield qualitative results (hopefully even quantitative ones), give immediate answers, and require nothing more than a chemical reagent, a sharp razor blade with which to section tissue, and a microscope.

I sent Louis off to the library in search of a chemical reagent specific for lead, one that would not react in the same way with any other metallic ions.

Louis, my Dr. Watson, brought one chemical agent after another into the lab for testing. We worked hard sectioning and soaking tissue, one batch of leaf and root tissue after another. I, Sherlock Holmes, scrupulously examined hundreds of slides under the microscope in a desperate attempt to detect the lead I knew must be present.

One day in his literature search Louis discovered that sodium rhodizonate was an excellent chromophoric agent for metallic ions. We thought we'd give it a try; perhaps it would bond with lead in a distinctive way.

I took precaution to section my lettuce leaf tissue especially thin. Louis prepared the chemical solution. We soaked the tissue, buffered it, washed off the excess stain, and mounted it on a slide. Sherlock took over. Under the microscope I scrutinized slide after slide. Suddenly, voila! There it was, big as life! At long last our tedious work had paid off.

"Louis," I shouted. "Louis, come quickly. Look."

Louis approached the microscope gingerly, looked through one ocular, and then, puzzled at my excitement said, "Dr. Glater, what do you see?"

"Can't you see, Louis? The lead's lit up bright red, in sharp contrast to the green chlorophyll-packed cells. It's dramatic! We did it! We did it!"

"Oh," Louis said sadly, "I'm so sorry. I'm red-green color blind."

Our paper was published in the *Air Pollution Control Association Journal,* Vol. 22, #6, dated June, 1972, a journal with an international distribution. We received over four hundred requests for reprints from all over the world. Obviously lead was a worldwide problem in all urbanized areas.

Louis, at my insistence, went on to finish a Ph.D. in organic chemistry at the University of California at Irvine. He was the first member of his hard-working Mexican family to be graduated from college, let alone receive a doctorate. Louis now has a lovely family and holds a prestigious position with a large research company in Albuquerque, New Mexico. I remained an untenured research associate in the School of Engineering at UCLA. But, although not particularly noticed or rewarded by the university, I had been successful in making some valuable scientific contributions to the study of air pollution. And I had been an inspiration for at least one worthwhile student (male, to be sure) to achieve academically.

An aside: One of the largest honors I ever received came in a letter from Louis dated February 2, 1981, several years after I had left the university. He had tracked me down in Santa Barbara. "I am finally getting married," he wrote, inviting me to his wedding. And, he added, "I wanted you to know that I was able to complete my studies for the Ph.D. because of the dedication to academic pursuit I learned from you." I was proud to attend his wedding. Never before or since have I shaken so many calloused, work-hardened hands as, with respect, he introduced his "professor" to each member of his large Mexican family and circle of friends.

While I was aware that my research may have been of some value, my spirits remained low throughout my tenuous stay at UCLA. I knew I was in the pocket of the male establishment with no way to climb out. With my whole heart I envied Dr. Flora Murray Scott. She had persisted in her fight for acceptance as a woman scientist, a fight she had won at the expense of her femininity. In those days, this seemed to be the price exacted of the few women who dared to aspire to so-called men's work. With men it was different. It was not necessary for them to choose between marriage and professional career. They could have both. And they were heartily encouraged (even pushed) in their quest for a professional identification.

From my days at UCLA I remembered a friend of Dr. Scott's, Dr. Barbara McClintock. On those occasions when she visited Scotty from Cold Spring Harbor in New York, one could often see the pair ambling down the hall to the coffee room, the diminutive, studious-looking Dr. McClintock in the shadow of the larger, more dominant Scotty. Both had a devotion to science above all else. Both dressed in a unisexual mode. Both eschewed marriage and the encumbrances of family. Both had been encouraged by their fathers to seek any career they desired. Gender did not seem to handicap them. Sadly, Scotty died alone in a total care facility in Santa Monica in the early '70s. I was advised not to visit her; she would not recognize me. Happily for all women scientists, Dr. McClintock, many years undercelebrated, finally won the Nobel prize in 1983 for her creative work in cytogenics. She died in 1992 at ninety, working until the end.

As part of my research under Prof. Vogt at UCLA I would often take trips into the fields of Los Angeles County to examine the crops. With each trip I became more aware that a new, different type of plant damage was displacing the old. Puzzled by this, I conjectured that perhaps the chemistry of the air was changing. On careful perusal of the chemical data, I saw that, indeed, the concentration of atmospheric nitrogen oxides had risen sharply and was continuing to rise daily. That was in the late 1960s. In the lab, I was successful in duplicating the new type of field damage by fumigating plants with the identical concentrations of oxides of nitrogen as were reported in the ambient air. But, try as I might, no academic journal would accept my research. Dr. Vogt, who had been in charge of my project had died, and my job was nearing its close. Unable to get my paper published, I consulted my new supervisor, Dean L.M.K. Boelter, who had taken over for Prof. Vogt to see the project to its imminent end. He said: "Let's publish it ourselves," and a UCLA School of Engineering Report #70-17 (March 1970) was printed and distributed to those scientists known by us to be doing research in air pollution. At best it had a limited distribution.

I skip ahead to December 14, 1991. I am now living in Santa Barbara. A news item in the Los Angeles Times *catches my eye. It quotes the National Academy of Sciences: "Data used in smog war challenged. Experts say air data flawed. For years it was assumed that most of the smog problem could be solved by controlling hydrocarbons.... But that approach was based on calculations that hydrocarbons in the air were ten times higher than oxides of nitrogen.... Efforts were misguided by targeting hydrocarbons alone. Far more control* should have been placed on nitrogen oxides." *The old melancholy overtakes me as I read. For hours, for days, I cannot shake my depression as my mind relives my final days at the university, when my work as a scientist had been shunted aside, my research trivialized. More than thirty years later, I feel the National Academy has finally vindicated me by corroborating my oxides of nitrogen studies.*

Parenting and Consequences _____

I had been married to Bud for three years and, although not taking measures to prevent it, had not yet become pregnant. I had no concept that my body, in its wisdom, was rejecting pregnancy. In my head I kept hearing the old familiar tape: "Get married, have children, forget career, cleave to husband." That is what my parents had taught me. That is what society dictated. That is the way I had been socialized. I was thirty-seven years old. If not now to have children, when? After a medical diagnosis of infertility and a series of doctor-administered hormonal injections, I surprised everybody, especially myself, by bearing first one daughter, Selina, then another, Sara, sixteen months later.

Selina was born on August 19, 1957, eight months after my thirty-eighth birthday, an unexpected, belated birthday present. She was born fully three months premature.

Soon after her untimely birth, my thoughts turned once again to my professional work. I wished to return to the university, but I found I could not in good conscience leave a newborn preemie at home in the hands of a babysitter. My husband went to work each day as head of the household and provider for the family. Baby care was not a man's responsibility; that was woman's work. No alternative came to mind; that was the way of the world. One day I had a thought. I would borrow a microscope and appurtenances from the university and set up a small lab for myself in the library at home. There I tried very hard to focus on my research but, without sleep due to Selina's inordinate need for care, I was able to manage only a few brief hours of concentration each day.

When Selina was nine months old, to my surprise and dismay, I was pregnant again, this time without benefit of medication. Sara was born sixteen months after Selina. Nor was hers a completely normal birth. In female matters I did not seem capable of normalcy. She was post-term. Two weeks after her due date the doctor induced labor, and on February 3, 1959, I gave birth to my second daughter.

After an absence of three years from the university, I felt anxious to return to my research. Selina was not quite three, Sara, one. By now my grant from the USPHS had expired and I was rehired as a research biologist in the School of Engineering. My job dictated that I was to work wherever my services were needed. I no longer had my own project, but worked on several different projects, under several different male professors. On one day I might be counting bacteria for Prof. Albert Bush on his sewage water conversion project; on another I might work for Dr. Sid Loeb on his project, *"Sea Water Demineralization by Means of a Semi-permeable Membrane"*; on yet another I might be working in air pollution under the supervision of Prof. Carl Vogt. My work was always subordinate; I was in complete charge of nothing.

In the '60s and '70s there were only four untenured women staff research associates in the School of Engineering with a faculty of more than 400 males. Dr. Catherine Wilson and I shared a laboratory. A top-notch chemist, she, like me, was research staff and untenured. So was Dr. Hilda Groth, a Ph.D. physiologist working as research associate in the biochemistry lab next door. None of us was in charge of her own project. We were used wherever we were needed. The fourth woman was a graduate engineer who was placed in charge of the steno-pool and publications office. She too was staff, not faculty.

Soon Hilda disappeared. She left her job. I suppose she could afford or wished to be unemployed. After many years, unable to obtain a faculty position at UCLA, Catherine left for a job with Stanford Research Institute. I hung on tentatively.

This was the hapless fate of professional women at that time in that place.

I am a responsible person. I tried hard to be all things to all people—a good mother, a good wife, a good scientist. But dividing myself between home and university was difficult. As the years wore on, my premature daughter's physical and emotional problems continued to worsen. Her nervous system could not overcome the insult of her having been rudely ejected from the womb three months too soon. As she grew older I sought help for her from all manner of therapists, social workers, play therapists, psychologist, and psychiatrists. In desperation I was forced to pull away from my professional work to care for her. Each day I, with Selina in tow, made visit upon visit to one type of mental health worker or another. But each day Selina grew worse. She withdrew more and more from her peers, from her sister, from me, and from her father. Slowly but surely, the fabric of the family that once was began to fray and unravel under the stress of my need to care for a very sick family member. My research at the university suffered as I attempted to deal with my domestic problems. The bulk of the household duties fell upon me. Although he helped as much as he could at home, Bud was obliged to work each day to earn a living. He did not complain, but I knew he was tired, and I sensed his growing anger, which he directed at me. On January 22, 1972, Selina, age fifteen, was institutionalized in Vista Del Mar Child Care Center in West Los Angeles. She remained there for three years, until she was eighteen.

Shortly after Selina's institutionalization, overcome by a sense of failure and worthlessness, I wrote in my diary:

By now I have outlived my usefulness to my husband. Through the past eighteen years that we have lived together as husband and wife, we have created a beautiful home, a monument to comfortable family living. We have added and altered rooms in the tiny house that we so confidently, purchased shortly after our marriage. Despite doctors' predictions that I would probably never have children, I conceived and bore two girls. It was a difficult uphill climb for me, but I persevered, by sheer will, to accomplish what most women do so easily. I wanted to be successful in my professional life but, failing that, I wished to be successful in the female domestic role, the only role I thought was left to me as a woman. Bud had an optimistic five-year plan for remodeling the house and, together, we achieved it. There are separate bedrooms for each girl, a large master bedroom and private bath for ourselves overlooking the garden, a beautiful pool with a large wooden patio, a lath-covered area over which trail beautiful wisteria vines, blooming once each year with a profusion of fragrant cascading lavender flowers. Under this lath where azaleas, camellias, and orchids flourish, we have kept cool on hot summer afternoons and the children have played. And there is the library with knotty pine walls, which Bud has so meticulously constructed around space left over when we pushed out the back wall of the house. There, amidst a profusion of books, I could sit on the small pumpkin-colored couch and enjoy a few moments of quietude and a good book.

Thus, ruminating with a broken heart, I relived eighteen years, and I knew instinctively that whatever had been gained in the domestic area was slowly ebbing away, and with it my hopes for a professional identity. My health began to fail seriously. In September 1969, one day after Yom Kippur, the Day of Atonement, I underwent open-heart surgery.

Post-surgery and recovery were difficult, physically and emotionally. Although I wrestled with weakness and despair, I was still devoted to family. I understood Bud's sadness, but I could not understand his ever-increasing rage at me. Life's tensions were pressing hard on both of us and pulling us apart. We were withdrawing more and more from one another, he from me more than I from him. Abruptly one day, without explanation or apology, he left home. This was the beginning of the end of my second marriage.

Twenty years had gone by, twenty years of useless psychoanalysis with Dr. Winter. The thrust of his treatment had been to convince me that I was an incomplete person, a mere female without a meaningful, attainable goal. My time with him begged for closure, long overdue.

At our very last session, the end of our relationship, he showed me a paper he had written, an extensive article on my case which he had presented, unbeknownst to me, at a national American Psychiatric Association meeting. The paper was entitled "The Psychoanalysis of a Scientist." It described me, not by name (thank God for small favors), thus:

"Her physical proportions were definitely feminine with ample bosom and well-padded hips, but her body was stiff and wooden. Her movements were awkward and she walked with a somewhat masculine stride."

I could not believe what I read! At home I looked long in the mirror. Then I probed my friends. Could this be true? Each said the same thing: "Not at all, not at all, quite the opposite."

In all those years the doctor knew only his own truth—that women are indeed subordinate to men because they lack a penis. That was what she is yearning for, he wrote in his paper describing my role as scientist. She suffers from penis-envy.

"Sometimes as she worked at her microscope she felt an almost uncontrollable surge of power within her. She felt power in her eyes, power in her hands, a tangible feeling of something like a penis between her legs."

A lie! An outrage! His words were a gross distortion of what I had spoken. The truth was that the gender possessing a penis, those who inhabited the halls of academia, those who were powerful, had banished me, and I was justifiably angry. What I wanted was a job worthy of my training. During our sessions, I had often complained, "I want a man-sized job," meaning not literally that I wished for a penis, but that I wished for equality.

Too late my suspicions were confirmed. Dr. Winter had indeed kept me on as a patient all those futile years in order to prove his own fast-held masculine theories, his own prowess as a superior male compared to me, a mere woman. The psychiatrist, whose job it was to facilitate my finding myself and my truth, had led me deeper and deeper into the darkness of untruth. He taught me to distrust the deep spiritual part of myself that, on one level, knew the reality that yearned for equality, freedom, and acceptance, but, on another level, did not know how to achieve it in the world he believed in, a world hostile to women. For years I had labored under the illusion that his frigidity was part of the analytic incognito, but no, his was a cold disinterest in my emancipation—probably in the emancipation of all women.

Eight months after my open-heart surgery, I began to feel ill again, worse with each passing day. Every two weeks I visited my cardiologist. My blood pressure was high, my pulse rapid, and I suffered anginal pain. I was told my bypass had failed! A new angiogram indicated that the right coronary artery, which had been replaced with a piece of the saphenous vein from my right leg, had again shut down. In addition, in the time that had elapsed, several other arterial blockages had occurred. Now the doctors claimed I was in need of a triple bypass. Another open-heart surgery? I was devastated.

There was no more good, giving father. He had died in 1965. There was no brilliant, if controlling, manipulative mother. She had died in 1972. And there was no supportive, loving brother. He had been killed in battle. Nor was there my psychiatrist of long years. He had proven himself useless. And now there was no husband who, in hostility, had gone to another woman. In my misery and aloneness, very close to the edge, I wept. "God, I am crying out to you for help. Can you hear my anguish? Am I not entitled to some consideration, though a woman?"

Awakening

Nothing before, nothing behind;
The steps of Faith fall on a seeming void
And find the rock beneath.

JOHN GREENLEAF WHITTIER

I have come to believe in miracles. From that desperate time on, in some inexplicable way, my life became a series of divine interventions. It was indeed a miracle that God heard my pleas, although, to be truthful, I was not yet aware of His intervention. All I could understand was that I had to take hold of life alone; that life itself was a miracle. Except for Selina, who had just been released from Vista Del Mar and was back living with me, I was alone. I could expect no help from her. She was still very fragile emotionally. Sara was at the University of California at Santa Cruz and visited me infrequently, briefly, and always angrily. Bud had gone to another woman. Carl Vogt, the professor under whose aegis I had been working at UCLA, died suddenly, and my job died with him. I needed work, a source of income. Bud had moved out of the house without making a financial commitment. Money would be forthcoming only after the divorce was finalized.

I searched everywhere on campus at UCLA, at local colleges, everywhere, anywhere; no teaching or research job was available to me. Soon, however, I found employment at the Veterans Administration in West Los Angeles doing research in plethysmography, a field about which I knew nothing and in which I had had no training. But I could learn. Using a plethysmograph, I was taught to determine the flow of blood into the occluded arteries of patients' legs. The job paid poorly, but at least I was earning some money and, in addition, I was acquiring a new skill.

I was one of a team studying the effects of cigarette smoking on male veterans who had been three-pack-a-day smokers for at least thirty years. At the V.A. hospital we were accumulating overwhelming evidence that heavy cigarette users suffered claudication, that is pain and lameness after walking short distances because the circulation to their legs had been severely compromised. Although our research was yielding important information, the federal government, in its wisdom, felt its money was better needed elsewhere. In the midst of the Cold War, money for military matters took priority over the health and welfare of our citizens. Suddenly President Ford cut the funding, and the project went belly-up. Goodbye, paycheck.

Before proceeding with my divorce, I thought it vital to distance myself from my unhappy domestic scene, if only for a short time. For all the years I had been Bud's wife, I had been tense, anxious, unable to travel, unable to leave home. It was time to test my new-found freedom. Perhaps, from afar, I might have better perspective on how to proceed with my life. I decided to go to Israel, to the land of my people. I had stashed away a bit of money from my short-lived V.A. job, enough to get me to Israel and back.

In March 1976, I boarded a plane from Los Angeles to New York on my way to Tel Aviv. Dr. Lefevre, my cardiologist, had put me on a regimen of stelazine, soritrate, propanalol, nitroglycerine, and God knows what else to help control my angina. My hands shook visibly from the medication, but I went bravely, knowing that I must have faith in myself. There was no room in my life for fear.

The trip across the Atlantic was uneventful but most encouraging. Although traveling alone, I was not one bit frightened, as I had been whenever traveling with Bud. There was no one to stare critically at me as he always did when we took a trip together. No one to judge me, to mock me if I were tremulous. I felt confidence in the new person I was becoming. And, more than that, I experienced no angina.

Dusk was falling as the El Al plane approached Ben Gurion Airport. A few Orthodox Jews, old men with long gray beards, had gathered at the rear of the cabin to pray the evening prayers, the *maariv*. At the same time, heart-stirring Israeli music filled the cabin. I felt like the wandering Jew who had finally returned to her land and her people after some 5,000 years. Overcome by emotion, tears streaming down my face, I left the plane. I stood all alone in a strange airport, in a strange land, people rushing past me in every direction. But I did not feel like a stranger in a strange land. Somehow, I felt at home and at peace.

As I stood there, not knowing where to go, I realized that I had not described my appearance to the tour company. How would I be recognized? I did not have time to worry long before a man approached me and, in a brusque manner, which I soon learned was the Israeli way, he said: "Glater?"

"Yes," I said. "How did you know my name?"

He did not bother to answer but picked up my two suitcases. "Follow me," he said. As we hustled through the airport, I saw a group of Arabs in their native attire, *kaffiyehs* bound around their heads and wearing their long, loose-fitting, hooded *djellabahs*, garb I had never seen before except in pictures. They were wildly gesticulating, shouting at one another in Arabic. I called to my guide, who was steps ahead of me by now, "What's going on?"

"Nothing, nothing to worry. There's always trouble with Arabs, probably drugs, maybe a horse to trade, who knows?" he tossed back over his shoulder, as we moved quickly on to a waiting car. He whisked me away to my home away from home, the beautiful Dan Hotel in Tel Aviv.

For the next two weeks I was up at six each morning, showered and dressed. In the dining room, from a long table laden high with fresh fruits, vegetables, and other simple foods, I picked up a couple of hard-boiled eggs, a few pieces of hard cheese, some cucumber slices, and an orange. Typical Israeli diet. Some of this I gulped down for breakfast. The rest I tucked into a paper sack to munch on along the way. Then hurriedly I descended to the lobby to await the tour bus. Several other American tourists were already in the minibus. We were eight in all, including our driver-tour guide. Each day, except for the Sabbath, we spent from early morning until nightfall exploring Israel—Cesarea, the Western Wall, Jerusalem, Tel Aviv, Bethlehem, the Negev, Sfad, the Knesset, the Druse village. It was a wonderful, exciting return to my ancient roots! I felt comfortable and happy. And I slept soundly. Still no angina.

I spent one Sabbath with my cousin Zvi Peretz Cohen and his family in Kiryat Ata. It was a traditional Orthodox Shabbat with the same *shalom beit* I remembered from my childhood. We talked about many things during the drawn-out Shabbat meal, kicking back, letting time run on its own. As a child, I had been raised to observe the Sabbath this way but, in the course of busy, passing years, had abandoned it. It was wonderfully relaxing to return to it now that my life was in such turmoil. When I return home, I thought, I must remember to set aside one day from the rest of the week to retrench, to thank God for the week that was, to gather energy to face the new. It was like prayer, like meditation. Sunday was the first day of the Israeli work week. At home in America Sundays were lost days to me, not particularly restful, myriad chores to be done. But here in Israel Sunday was at the head of the week, a new invigorating workday following the peace and relaxation of the Shabbat.

After two weeks of non-stop touring, I was ready to return to America. I thought I might like to make my permanent home there in Israel but, back in California, my life was on hold. I didn't know whether Bud had changed his mind and returned home to me, or whether I would want him if he had. And what would become of Sara and Selina should I stay? No, as I walked the streets of Haifa I knew it was not yet time to make a drastic move. Later I would see. Now I was anxious to get on with it, to face whatever awaited me. At the Western Wall in Jerusalem, just before leaving Israel, I wrote a *kvitel*, a small note on a tiny piece of paper, which I folded carefully and inserted into a crevice between the ancient Temple rocks. On it I wrote, "God give me the strength to do what I must." Whatever it was I had to do upon my return, I now knew I had the courage to do. I had touched base with my ancient roots, my heritage, and I was renewed.

Selina picked me up at LAX upon my return. Bud showed up at the house to greet me, stayed a few minutes, said nothing, and quickly vanished. I knew when I saw him that there was no hope of reconciliation. I had learned by now that I was capable of handling life on my own. I could travel. I could be away from home. I could enjoy life. Alone, without Bud, I felt strong. Now, in his presence, I could once again feel the old sick dependency creeping back. I would have none of that. Reasons for my enervating reaction to him no longer mattered. What mattered was that I now had confidence in myself. Renewed and clear, I began the work I knew I must do— rid myself once and for all of this marriage.

Fortunately, I found Nancy Weston, a marriage, family, and child counselor (MFCC) who worked on the counseling staff at UCLA and also had a private practice close to campus.

Nancy was a pretty, young woman, much younger than I, divorced, raising two daughters alone. She, unlike Dr. Winter, listened and heard my pain, interacted with me, joined me in laughter and in tears. She was honest and open about herself and her own problems and encouraged me to speak freely about mine. With her gentle, firm support, I soon learned that I possessed the innate intelligence as well as the emotional strength to go it alone. Early on, she made two recommendations that sped me on my road to recovery: (1) that I get a competent divorce attorney, one who would act quickly and aptly, and get the job done and over; and, (2) that I learn to practice some form of meditation, any kind. "Relax," she said, "You must relax."

When I left her office after one of my early meetings, I went to the Transcendental Meditation center, a few doors from her office, and made an appointment to learn the technique of meditating. Although skeptical of the process, I was willing to try anything—I was fighting for the rest of my life. Then I called the attorney Nancy had suggested and set up an appointment.

With Nancy's help, the sad course of my life began to change. She made yet one further suggestion; she wanted Bud to attend one of our sessions, for the three of us to talk. I called him at work, and he agreed to come.

That meeting was a moment of truth for me. Nancy encouraged both of us to talk. I spoke accusingly. He countered defensively. My temper flared. I called him a cheat and a liar. I no longer respected him. I was sorry I had remained with his duplicity all those years. I hated his denigration of me as a woman and as a scientist. I hated his smug male superiority. I had never before had the courage to confront him. I had never before understood my own anger. As I spoke, my hostility became clear. For the first time I could see how intense my rage was, not only at him but also at the male-chauvinist psychiatrist Winter. And also at the entire male-dominated society that had penalized me for my gender and denied me my place in the world. Until that moment I knew only that I, married to Bud and "cared for" by Winter, had grown more unhappy each day. It was a relief to understand and speak aloud my rage, rage that for so long had been *verborgen*, buried deep within my heart, unspoken.

When Bud left, Nancy summed it up: "Ruth, you must let him go. Can't you see you are running circles around him? He can't possibly keep up with you. He needs to leave for safer ground. You can make it alone."

I could not remain at home without work. I was lonely,

though not for Bud, worried about my finances, and apprehensive about the outcome of the divorce, about sick Selina's future, and about my pending second heart surgery. Work had always been able to distract (if not fulfill) me. But I was not physically able to hold a full-time job even if I could find one.

I asked Ron Cooper, my attorney, if there was some work I could do at his office. He and three other attorneys shared a thriving law practice in a skyscraper in Century City, close to my home. He agreed to hire me as a receptionist and switchboard operator for five hours a day. The pay was minimal, but I would have accepted any salary for the opportunity to be with people, to feel useful, and to be out in the world doing honest work. No work was too menial for me.

The switchboard, as do any and all machines, baffled me. I could not learn to handle incoming and outgoing calls. I could not figure out how to transfer calls from one lawyer to another when that was necessary. My inability to cope with Ron's relatively simple switchboard might be explained, at least in part, by my preoccupation with my pending open-heart surgery. I was certain of my death should I undergo a second such operation. And, once again, a miracle occurred. God was indeed watching over me. This time He sent me Norma Schenk.

While in junior high school, Selina had made friends with her cooking teacher, Ms. Norma Schenk. As a result, I came to know this caring, gentle lady and remained friendly with her even after Selina left the school. To this woman I owe my life.

Norma was a maiden lady who taught cooking, nutrition, table-setting, and related subjects at Palms Junior High. She had a superb sense of beauty and design regarding the preparation and serving of foods. She knew the proper place settings, floral table arrangements, napkin folding, tablecloths, silverware, and everything necessary for elegant entertaining. She was indeed an artist who worked diligently to instill a sense of grace in the children. Selina, having a strong artistic bent, took to Norma immediately, and she to Selina.

One day I received a call from Norma. "Ruth," she said in her halting, measured way. "I have some news for you." She had attended a meeting of cooking teachers of Los Angeles schools the night before. Nathan Pritikin had been the guest speaker. "Have you heard of him?" she asked.

"No, I haven't," I said.

"Well, he spoke about people like you, people who have gone through one open heart surgery and, shortly thereafter, faced another. He claims the situation can be handled simply with diet and exercise rather than with drastic life-threatening surgery. I took the liberty of taping his speech, with his permission, of course. Would you like the tape?"

An alternative to surgery? My heart leaped up.

I listened to the tape again and again, several times a day for several days. Pritikin was not a dynamic lecturer, but once I heard and understood his message, I became very excited.

Dr. Rod Smith, the surgeon who had already scheduled me for a second open-heart surgery, was a tall, heavy-set man who, judging by his weight, did not believe in diets of any sort. "Tell ya," he said, "I know something about Pritikin's diet program. Ain't nobody can sustain life on it. Impossible. Awful tasting. You'll starve to death. Forget it."

Undaunted, hoping against hope for a reprieve from the knife, I returned to my cardiologist. "Tim, I need more information. Rod is thumbs down on Pritikin. Do you know any other bona fide cardiologist who might have better knowledge of Pritikin's program?"

"There's one fellow I know," he said, "Ben Rosin. He's chief of cardiology at Torrance Memorial Hospital and a professor at USC med school. He seems interested in Pritikin. Give him a call."

I did, and set up an appointment to see him at Torrance Memorial Hospital on April 12, 1977. I had to wait three weeks before he had time to see me.

During that time, Norma and I took a trip to Santa Barbara to visit the Pritikin Clinic at the Mar Monte Hotel. We had a meal there, and I spoke with Dr. Mannerberg, cardiologist to the program. He gave me some literature describing the Longevity Clinic and its work. The pamphlet contained several days' diet menus. "Try following this plan for a couple of weeks," he said. "In addition, do as much walking as you can, to the point of anginal pain. If you see any improvement, any improvement whatsoever, you'll be a candidate for this program. If not, see your surgeon immediately." I left with the absolute intention of making Pritikin's program work.

The day Norma and I arrived in Santa Barbara, the city was bathed in sunshine. The peaceful blue ocean was visible just outside the windows across the boulevard from the hotel. The clean, people-free beach was so different from the crowded Santa Monica beaches I knew. When I tasted the food in the clinic, I did not like it. It was fat-free, salt-free, taste-free. Maybe Rod Smith was right. Maybe the food was inedible. But I would try anything rather than submit to another surgery!

Upon my return home, I went shopping for vegetables, fruits, and grains. With my very next meal, I began to follow the prescribed eating plan. Almost immediately, I felt some relief from angina. Encouraged, I adhered strictly to the Pritikin diet for the next three weeks. Then I went to see Dr. Ben Rosin.

The divorce proceedings on November 5, 1976, were painful, as are those of most long marriages. As I started conferences with Ron Cooper, my attorney, I could hear the bell tolling the imminent death of my marriage. So many sad, futile, wasted years! Ron was on a roll. He moved fast and incisively, like a sharp blade. And it was over. Bud and I were granted joint custody of Sara, who was seventeen years old and still a minor, though living away from home at the University of California at Santa Cruz. Selina was eighteen and could choose to live wherever and with whomever she wished.

Spousal support was designated, commencing November 15, 1976, and continuing until my remarriage or the death of either party. The divorce was over...except for the six-month waiting period before final documents would be sent to me by the court.

The day after the court hearing I sat meditating, my mind replaying my long twenty-two-year-marriage. Then I wrote the following in my diary as if I were reciting my story to a listening, caring world:

It is the morning of November 6, 1976. I finally have my freedom. I am fifty-seven years and nine months old. I have a critical heart condition. If Pritikin's program fails me, I face a life-threatening triple-bypass heart surgery. It will be my second open-heart. I may not survive. I have two daughters. Selina is now eighteen, Sara, seventeen. Sara is at college in Santa Cruz. Selina is not well. She has never been well, not since birth, not from the moment she kicked a hole in my womb, broke the water, and saw the light of day as a six-month-old fetus. She had no business outside the womb, not for another three months. Her nervous system was not yet properly honed, not capable of handling life outside the womb. As a result, she has spent much of her short life with psychiatrists, therapists, and in psychiatric hospitals. But to little avail.

Sara has withdrawn from me. She does not understand why her father and mother have divorced. As far as she knew, everything was fine except for her sister's strange behavior. Now she is a student at the University of California at Santa Cruz. She feels alone and angry. When she comes to visit me, I complain. I speak of my illness. I speak of fear of my pending surgery. I speak of imminent death, which I do not want. I speak of anger against her father, who has abandoned me in my hour of need. It is not pleasant for Sara to see me like this or hear my complaints, so she curtails her visits. Sara loves her father. She is romantic, sensitive, impressionable. Her fa-

ther says he could not help himself from leaving me. He had fallen out of love with me, had fallen in love with another woman. Our beautiful home on Kelton Avenue is no longer his home. It has become a prison for him. He can no longer tolerate sharing his life with me. Too much unhappiness. Too much sickness. He says he is not at fault, not to blame. It is heart-rending for him to give up the beautiful house he built almost entirely with his own hands. All the money he expended on it, too! All the memories he has of his children growing up in it. Their laughter. Their tears. And at one time I thought we loved one another, he and I. We were mindful of one another's needs. Sara is touched by his words, by his sad, tearful complaints. She is moved by the absolution he grants himself. She loves him. She loved me, too, at one time, but I had gone away, had sequestered myself in my misery. He has told her this. She hears him and weeps, though not for me. Bud and his new love visit Sara often in the north. Sara has accepted Bud's woman as her new mother. I am no longer part of her life. Her rare visits to me are unpleasant for both of us. And she hates Selina and doesn't wish to ever see her. But being with her father and his new family is fun and freedom. Her father's love for his woman is new and fresh, and Sara has caught his excitement. I must now pick up the pieces of my life. I will not lie here and die.

Three weeks had gone by. I was on my way to see Dr. Rosin. It was a long freeway ride south to Torrance. Unknown territory had always made me nervous. I had never before been in Torrance. I was afraid of what the doctor might tell me.

The hospital was a bustling place surrounded on all sides by wide-open, undeveloped land. The cardiology department was in the basement of the hospital. I walked through what seemed to be endless narrow hallways cluttered with all sorts of medical equipment and finally arrived, breathless, excited, and apprehensive, at the doctor's tiny office at the end of a long corridor.

Dr. Rosin was sitting behind his desk. As I entered he stood up and extended his hand to greet me. I was amazed by his appearance. He was a huge, muscular, athletic man, not an ounce of fat on his body. This man, I thought, looks like an all-star quarterback rather than a doctor. He could have been intimidating as he towered over me except that, when he spoke, his voice and manner were soft and gentle. I liked him instantly. A gentle giant.

I described my symptoms and finished with: "I feel considerably better after having followed the Pritikin diet for three weeks. I can now walk about a block without angina."

Dr. Rosin, having finished his physical examination, urged me to go to Santa Barbara and try the Pritikin program before considering further surgery. "Yes," I said, "I certainly would like to do that, but all of my assets are frozen. My divorce settlement isn't complete yet. Essentially, I'm very short of money." He nodded as I spoke, indicating that he understood.

At that moment, a thought struck me. "But, Dr. Rosin," I said excitedly, "do you think Pritikin might be interested in my working on the program with him? I have had better than twenty years of post-doctoral research—true, not in the field of nutrition, but in botany, and his program is almost strictly vegetarian, isn't it? I wonder...." He had been making his way toward the door, ready to dismiss me, but he turned back when I spoke. "You know, that's not a bad idea," he said. "I know Pritikin. I'll give him a call."

Two days later, as I tended (or mal-tended) the switchboard at Ron Cooper's office, the phone rang. "Law offices," I said. "Is Ruth Glater there?" a man's voice asked. It was Nathan Pritikin. This time I managed not to cut off the caller.

Pritikin was blunt. "Dr. Rosin spoke to me about you a few days ago," he said. "Are you interested in beans?"

"Well, yes," I said, "but what do you mean?"

"I mean beans as a food source, as a source of protein."

"Yes," I answered, "I'm interested in anything that grows. If it's a plant, I'm interested."

"Okay," he said, "why don't you arrange to come here to Santa Barbara. You can go through the program and stay on to work off your fee. We'll see where to go from there."

Quick. Impersonal. Decisive. A man of very few words.

I was ecstatic. Maybe I had a few more years to live. Maybe even a new life. This was all unplanned, serendipitous. Yet another gift, another miracle.

In May 1977, I arrived in Santa Barbara to begin the next phase of my life. The divorce over, I still might, hopefully, have some good years left.

Many months following our ugly divorce, when the thick mud had settled, I realized that Bud had indeed saved my life by leaving. A stone had fallen from around my neck. My heart felt light. I had wanted out of my misery but had not knnow the way. But as Job had spoken to God millennia before, I now spoke to God:

God,
I know that You can do everything
that no place is impossible for You
Indeed I have been speaking sad words without under-
standing
Of things beyond me which I did not know.
Hear now and I will speak aloud
I will ask, and You will inform me.

This new insight freed me to become the person I truly was. Understanding filled my eyes. I began to see the clear path ahead. It took much study of the Book of Job to free me. It took concentration, meditation, prayer, and tears. But ultimately I surrendered to a Wisdom greater than my own, to a Strength beyond my own. And my new understanding began to lead me out of the darkness of despair into life-sustaining light.

•

Selina would often drive north from Santa Monica to visit me in Santa Barbara. She was still quite unsettled emotionally but seemed in better control of herself than ever before. Occasionally I drove south to Los Angeles to visit her and stay a few days. We remained in close contact with one another. But Sara, somewhere in northern California, did not communicate with Selina or with me. She was lost to both of us.

As a patient at the Pritikin Clinic, I attended lectures, ate bland, unseasoned nutritional food, which I found unpalatable at first and later learned to like, walked miles at a time, met many people as sick as I, received excellent medical attention, lived for a month in a beautiful room at the Mar Monte Hotel overlooking the blue Pacific, slept soundly, meditated, and had leisure time. For the first time in more than twenty-three years, I felt at peace. Nothing concerned me except my health. Each day, as my weight dropped, I felt as if I were coming back to life, like a wilted plant given water and sunlight. And Nathan Pritikin, testing me to see if he could eventually use me on staff, assigned me small tasks. I began to have a sense of self again, of being able to help myself, and a wish to help others. If I couldn't be a professor, the dream I had long since been forced to abandon, possibly I could be useful to society in a new way.

When I had finished the month-long program at the clinic, Nathan Pritikin, apparently satisfied, offered me a job lecturing to the patients on nutrition as well as doing library research for him. I was feeling quite well, had lost twenty pounds, and was now walking four miles a day. My second heart surgery had been cancelled. Pritikin offered me a generous salary. I took a month's leave to return to Los Angeles to dispose of my house and furniture and make arrangements for other living space for Selina. The house sold easily. A yard sale relieved me of all the household possessions I did not intend to take north with me, memories I did not wish to hold.

When I returned to Santa Barbara, I rented a one-bedroom furnished apartment at Por la Mar Circle, an apartment complex across the street from the Mar Monte, where I worked. It was simply but adequately furnished. And it was affordable, most unusual for Santa Barbara. Having come out of a large, ten-room house, it was amazing that I could be content in so small a space. But it was conveniently close to work and, in addition, I was permitted to take all my meals at the clinic. I had only to exit my front door to be at the shore, able to take my daily walks. Everything seemed fortuitously to have fallen in place. But I still felt some need for help with my bruised and battered emotions.

I started weekly sessions with a social worker. Although I was happier with my life than I had been in years, very absorbed in work, which was both enjoyable and rewarding, and feeling considerably better physically, I must admit to moments of intense anger at having been forced to abandon what I had long thought was permanent security with home, husband, and family. I had lost my ten-room meticulously appointed home, my pool, my tenderly cared-for garden, and my family status. I still had a great deal of residual anger for the way life had treated me, and for all the grief marriage had caused me. For the next year, I worked with Miriam, an expert therapist, letting go bit by bit.

During the day I was busy with people at the clinic. At night I returned to the quiet of my nest, the small apartment which served as my shelter from old pain. In fact, I was so ensconced in my thoughts, that when the historic fire of 1977 occurred in Sycamore Canyon in the hills above Santa Barbara, just above my apartment complex, a fire which destroyed hundreds of expensive homes, I was not aware of the terrible tragedy, of the billowing smoke, of the sirens shrieking throughout the night. It was not until morning, when I returned to work, that I learned what had happened. How could I have been so out of touch with the horrible reality that was occurring just outside my windows? The explanation lay in the fact that I was exhausting myself in my work, building a new life, and trying hard to bury the past.

I am indebted to Nathan Pritikin for the education he permitted me to receive while paying me a good salary. I am most grateful for the ease with which he accepted me, without prejudice, though a woman, and assigned me the important job as director of food and agriculture research in his clinic. In return, I may have contributed something to the success of his program. I hope so.

The nutrition program Pritikin promoted was far ahead of the medical community's dietary knowledge at the time. In 1979, doctors and medical schools were paying little attention to diet and exercise. Medical students were being given barely more than a single course in nutrition as part of their four-year training. But why were so many doctors reluctant to hear Nathan's story? Evidence that his program worked was becoming clearer with each group of patients successfully treated at the clinic. But there were only a few cardiologists like Dr. Rosin who were open to what Pritikin was saying. Today the medical profession has accepted programs like his as an alternative to open-heart surgery. And many life-threatening surgeries have been averted. The possibility of a natural reversal of arterial blockages in response to appropriate diet and exercise is now an acknowledged fact, although when Pritikin suggested it in the 1970s, it was pooh-poohed by most of the medical establishment.

One morning, just as I was arriving to work, I ran into Nathan. He was leaving the front door for his daily jog. He stopped me; I thought he meant to chastise me for my tardiness. Instead, to my relief, he said: "Ruth, what do you know about smog in Los Angeles?"

He was aware of my former research in air pollution. "Well," I said, thinking he was asking out of interest in the matter, "as you know, the air in Los Angeles is heavily polluted. People with emphysema or cardiovascular disease should not live there. If, for one reason or another, one must live there, the only place that is relatively safe is at the shore, like perhaps the beach at Santa Monica or Malibu."

He beamed, something he rarely did. I had no idea he had anything more in mind than a passing interest in smog. "Thanks," he said, "you've made my day." And off he jogged. I didn't know until several weeks later that I had innocently struck a death knell for the Santa Barbara clinic.

Unbeknownst to any of his employees, least of all to his Santa Barbara business administrator, Pritikin was surreptitiously negotiating with a millionaire from Ojai for the purchase of the old Synanon building near the pier at Santa Monica. Synanon had gone belly-up, and their building lay abandoned at the beach and in total disarray. For six million dollars it could be had, building, shore-front, land, and all. The millionaire from Ojai was willing to put up the money, or a large part of it, to "buy in." While on the one hand Nathan was secretly dealing with his prospective partner, he had, on the other hand, given his business administrator orders to negotiate with the owner of the Mar Monte Hotel in Santa Barbara for more rental space. The administrator, having been told nothing of the Santa Monica deal, had been working long, hard hours with the Mar Monte's owner to draw up a satisfactory contract. Little did he know that Nathan was working both ends against the middle.

Suddenly, Nathan called an emergency meeting of the entire staff and announced that the clinic was being moved to Santa Monica in only two weeks. He and his mysterious benefactor had reached an agreement.

We were about eighty people on staff at the time, including receptionists, physical therapists, nutritionists, health educators, and doctors, all of us in turmoil.

"No problem," Nathan said, "you can all move to the new Santa Monica clinic, and you will receive a twenty percent pay raise."

But most families, especially those with children, could not uproot themselves on such short notice. As for me, I had just sold my house in west Lost Angeles, two miles from the newly proposed Santa Monica clinic, and had purchased a home in Santa Barbara. I could not move back now. Nor did I wish to.

We all banded together and an army of stunned employees descended upon the Pritikin mansion in Montecito. In the foyer outside his huge, handsome living room, expensively furnished with antiques, thick carpets, and opulent lamps, we stood huddled in a crowd, dismayed, bewildered, and outraged by his deceit. Standing before us, his wife hiding sheepishly behind him, he insisted the clinic would move in two weeks. No amount of pleading, no amount of angry confrontation could move him. He was not to be deflected. His mind was made up!

"What about the contract I have drawn up with the Mar Monte?" his business administrator called from the crowd.

"Sorry," Pritikin said, "Tear it up. You signed it. I didn't."

On the sad day the clinic moved, we who remained behind stood helplessly by, watching the furniture, equipment, and files go. There were tears. We were sorry to see the Santa Barbara clinic close. We loved the program. It had been good to us and to the patients as well. Actually, only one or two Santa Barbara employees moved to Santa Monica, although they did not receive the promised twenty percent increase. The others of us scattered in the wind.

For a few months after the move, I was invited to deliver a biweekly nutrition lecture at the new Santa Monica clinic. That is, until Pritikin hired a new full-time nutritionist. And then I was no longer needed.

I had a new house and a new way to earn a living, but I had no job. True, my degrees were not in the field of nutrition, but I had acquired invaluable hands-on experience at the clinic and had garnered much information from reading and studying while working there. I knew the Pritikin program like the back of my hand. I lived it. I believed in it. Using the tenets of the program, I could now teach and help others to help themselves toward health. I knew my knowledge was marketable. I had only to find someone who could use me.

A few days after Pritikin fired us, I was interviewed for a job as nutrition consultant to a newly formed health group. David Doner, M.D., and Bruce Gladstone, Ph.D., had just opened a health practice on Fletcher Avenue across the street from Cottage Hospital. They were both highly trained governors in the Maharishi's Transcendental Meditation program and were interested in hiring a nutritionist who was also a meditator. Dr. Doner was an internist with a specialty in nephrology, and Dr. Gladstone a Ph.D. in psychology with a strong bent toward behavior modification. Although they had no formal training in nutrition, both were aware of the importance of diet and exercise. Because I had worked with Pritikin, held a Ph.D., and was a meditator to boot, they hired me on the spot. I was paid twenty dollars per consultation, part of which I had to pay back to them for the use of their space.

I did this work successfully for several months. However, my good fortune did not last. Gladstone, the business head of the young organization, not yet busy in his own practice, decided to do my work as well as his. I was let go. So I was out of work again.

My new house, high in the hills above Santa Barbara, did not meet my needs. Stores and shopping were not easily accessible. The roads up to the house were tortuous and dark, making homecoming in the night dangerous. I sold the house as soon as I could and bought a condominium on the east side of Santa Barbara, close to downtown, close to all amenities.

Letting Go

It had been years of long, hard struggle. It was time to enjoy what was left of my time on earth, I thought. I could afford to retire if I was frugal. I was in my early sixties and emotionally and physically weary of frenetically trying to find work. Instead I decided to busy myself with good friends and attending lectures and cultural events, doing things I could not do if working. I began to live an interesting, involved, and active life. I knew it was certainly too late to pursue any career—either in science or in marriage. And, as I ceased my struggle to find my place in the world, my life began to improve and unfold like the petals of a sweet-scented flower.

One of the first "letting-go" things I did was to take a trip to the British Isles. The Adult Education Division of Santa Barbara City College offered such a trip, reasonably priced— practically wholesale. My friend Charlotte Pritikin and I decided to join the group. (Charlotte was Nathan's sister-in-law; we had remained good friends even after the clinic moved.)

For the first two weeks we visited many places—London, the Lake Country, Stratford-on-Avon, Glasgow, Edinburgh. Charlotte was a great travel companion, unhurried, undaunted. Even when she sprained her ankle getting off a British bus, she hobbled all the rest of the way through Europe without complaint. We were carefree and content. She is gone now, and I miss her.

The third week of our trip was less enjoyable. Unlike the other members of our Santa Barbara group, who had already departed for home, Charlotte and I purchased an additional week's tour of France, Holland, Belgium, and Germany. We foolishly bought the most inexpensive tour we could find, thinking we had made a huge bargain. Instead, to our chagrin, we found the opposite was true. Our bargain put us up in the poorest hotels in each of the countries we visited. And they were indeed poor!

In Amsterdam, our hotel had a communal women's bathroom with a dozen shower stalls in a straight row. I hesitantly entered the shower stall. I could think only of the German death camps, afraid to turn the faucets on lest lethal gas escape from the jets.

As we traveled by bus through Germany, I had the eerie feeling that the Gestapo was still operating, watching me, ready to throw yet another miserable undesirable into a concentration camp. The bus driver, obviously German, turned on loud military marching music as we sped across the countryside, the road skirting the Black Forest. I began to weep softly. I imagined blood dripping from every tree—the blood of Jews. Diffidently, I asked the driver to turn off the music. "Please," I said, "I have a bad headache." He gruffly refused me. Did he know I was a Jew? Was he a Nazi in a bus driver's uniform?

Our bus tour stopped to spend the night in a picturesque little inn in a rural German hamlet. Before dinner, with a bit of time to spare, I took a walk. A short way up the unpaved country road, I came upon a church with a stone marker dated 1690 A.D. The two steps leading up to the large, wooden front doors were worn down by the footsteps of the many, many parishioners who must have entered the church over its three-hundred-year life. I tried the door; I wished to enter, to pray for my fellow Jews who had perished. Some of them might have once lived in this very village. But the door was locked. However, not to be deprived of expressing my anguish, I stood on the church steps and, in a loud voice, my words shattering the stillness, I called out to God: "*Shmah Yisrael, Adonai eloheinu, Adonai echad....* Hear, O Israel, the Lord our God, the Lord is One." These must have been the words on the lips of every Jew as he or she was herded onto a cattle car en route to a concentration camp, and the very last words as he or she entered the gas chamber en route to eternity. And, in this place of horrible visions for me, where no person heard my prayer, I wondered why I had chosen to visit Germany and swore never to return.

Shortly after returning home, I went to see Dr. Bobgan, dean of Adult Education at Santa Barbara City College. It was he who had been our director on the British Isles tour. He understood my zeal when I asked him if I might be permitted to teach a course in nutrition. We had been served a very unhealthful diet abroad and, on many occasions, he and I had discussed what seemed to be British disregard for proper nutrition, certainly in those places we had visited. He heartily accepted my proposal to teach. Once again I had a job—one that was small and paid little—but was very satisfying.

Starting in 1979 I taught several courses in nutrition: The Perplexed Eater—A Mini-course in Nutrition; Some Practical Guidelines for Healthful Weight Management; The Human Need for Calcium; What's New in Nutrition—Current Research; and The Perplexed Dieter—Permanent Healthful Weight Loss. I used what knowledge I had acquired while on my job with Pritikin. In addition I had added to my knowledge by continuing to read in nutrition.

I truly enjoyed the classroom and the interaction with the attentive adult students. But unfortunately, by May 1982, I could no longer do my work. I had proposed a new course, Fit Food for Fit Folk—A Study of Foods, which I looked forward to teaching, but by then my left hip was in such severe agony from arthritis that I could no longer stand on my feet. Teaching a two-hour class, even once a week, had become impossible. The pain was unrelenting. Anti-inflammatory drugs helped less and less. At night I would awaken to pain shooting up and down my left leg, pain that felt like sharp claws ripping at my flesh. The time had come for drastic measures.

Surgery was inevitable.

In February 1983, I had a total hip replacement on the left side. A few years later, my right arthritic hip gave up the ghost and I was the reluctant recipient of yet another replacement. I am today a bionic woman, walking slowly and cautiously on two totally reconstructed hips.

In 1982 Selina moved from Los Angeles to Santa Barbara, and my peace was rudely shattered. From birth, she had suffered incurable bipolar disease, and still did. After graduation from Pepperdine University she came to Santa Barbara to attend graduate school at UCSB and soon found quarters in university housing near campus. For the next five years, until her graduation in 1987, she leaned heavily on me for financial and emotional support. Between her frequent bouts of mental illness she courageously attended classes, but at a slow pace. It was a difficult time for both of us. In 1987 she finally graduated with honors from UCSB with a master's degree in musicology.

Shortly thereafter, she obtained an excellent job as director of cultural and performing arts for the Jewish Community Center in Dallas, Texas. From the moment she arrived there, she missed home and friends and the familiar surroundings of California. Or perhaps the job was too stressful for her. After a few weeks, she once again fell apart emotionally and was confined to a psychiatric hospital in Dallas. Several months later, when she returned to Santa Barbara, I picked her up at the Greyhound station on Carrillo Street.

She looked drawn, pale, sick. Her hair was long and matted, her clothes dirty and unkempt. She wept as she related the story of her hospitalization. She chastised me for being heartless, for not being there for her like a loving, caring mother should have been. I was never there for her, she scolded, not since she was a child, not ever. But this was patently untrue; her demands had always been inordinate, impossible to gratify. They still were. My heart broke for both of us, for what she could not get from life and for the health and strength I could not give her.

Upon her return to Santa Barbara, I felt myself sinking deeper and deeper into hopelessness. There seemed to be no end to her misery, nor to that which she heaped on me. At first she lived under my roof. It was impossible, like two cats in a sack. She soon moved into her own apartment, out of my house, though not out of my life. After much travail, she now works as an advocate for the mentally ill with the County of Santa Barbara Mental Health Services, a job for which she is well suited. It is my hope that her life will continue to smooth out as science finds more answers and more efficient drugs to help cope with manic-depressive illness.

If my story were to end here, it would indeed be a sad one: two failed marriages, one daughter alienated, another suffering crippling emotional illness, an academic career long since aborted, aspirations dashed, physical health impaired, onrushing years weighing heavily upon me and dragging me down. And I was alone.

With all these seeming failures, it was difficult to keep perspective, though miraculously, despite it, I hung in and kept my life moving quietly, more or less peacefully, forward. I must admit to moments of extreme sadness when from time to time I would recall my shattered dreams, especially on those occasions when I saw men far less well trained and capable than I retiring into financial security, after having completed successful academic careers. And they had done it with such ease. I could not help feeling that life had cheated me. But those moments of self-pity were few. I could rise above them.

One day I decided to do something that I had for many years wanted to do. I would take a cruise to Alaska, a new frontier. The thought excited me. At that point in my life, I craved a new adventure. Here was a chance to see God's untrammeled world before it became too late, before man destroyed it, before I totally lost my physical ability to travel.

With fear and trepidation lest my ersatz hips fail me, I purchased my ticket. Happily the trip went remarkably well. I was able to manage the gangplank, although cautiously, at each and every port of call. Alaska was as breathtaking as I thought it would be. It was a new, expansive world with relatively few inhabitants to sully it. And I felt a strong sense of accomplishment at having been physically able to make such a long, difficult trip…and so enjoyably.

The crowning jewel of this exhilarating trip came one bright, sunny day when the seas were extremely rough. Although the keel of our ship was deep (deeper than any other ship's keel, the S.S. *Universe* brochure bragged), which should have steadied her, she kept pitching and rolling. My stomach rolled with her. There is nothing like seasickness to make one want to die. At such a time, life seems not worth the effort.

As I sat at the lunch table toying with my food, unable to eat, one of the guests advised me to look out the porthole and keep my eye on the steady horizon. Let me assure you that is not the way to stabilize oneself. The horizon is not steady as the boat heaves and plunges through the water. There is no straight line on which to fix one's eyes. A wiser person advised me to go outside and lie flat on my back on a deck chair, close to the rail.

I went topside. Flat on my back, the rail steadied me a bit as I clung to it for support. Just then, from the sky descended the most glorious sight my eyes had ever beheld. It was a large, fawn-colored bird, its wingspread about eight feet. She dropped gracefully from the sky and flew past me as I lay motionless on my chair. She came so close, I could have touched her. Effortlessly, gracefully, she flew past me, soared, circled around, and came back yet again. Her feathers were deep velvet; her grace, her ease of motion were breathtaking. Here was a divine sight. I forgot nausea. I forgot the wish to die. I forgot myself as I gloried in the magnificence of this heavenly creature.

Later, when checking with the Audubon Society, I learned

I had been privileged to see a very rare sight indeed, an albatross. Few people, I was told, had ever come that close to one.

At the time I wanted so much to touch the bird as she swooped past me, but it felt sinful to defile, even by touch, such an exquisite creature. What a spectacular sight! What a fantastic cure for seasickness! I believed that God, from His place in heaven, had sent the albatross directly to me as a promise of good things yet to come. I kept this hope locked in my heart all the way home to Santa Barbara.

My euphoria was short-lived, however. Upon my return Selina, living in her apartment close by mine, was still unrelenting in her dependency. Although she had a good job, her demands for my time and attention felt like a death-grip. I dreaded hearing from her lest it be yet another urgent request, impossible for me to meet. The pleasure of my beautiful Alaskan voyage began to recede as I struggled each day to maintain balance. With each new onslaught I felt myself sinking deeper and deeper into despair, my emotional life raft unable to support both her and me. I had by now exhausted the mental health capabilities at the Veterans Administration in Santa Barbara. The friendly, conscientious psychologist, Dr. Painter, who attended me there could do little more than hold my hand, and he could not do that forever. So when he told me he was dismissing me, I was worried. Could I make it alone without his support? Fortunately, at that very moment, as had happened at other low points in my life, a lifeline was thrown to me from Somewhere Out There. A friend had had a positive experience with a group called "The Families of Depressives Anonymous." He suggested I try it.

The Families of Depressives Anonymous turned out to be a twelve-step program patterned after Alcoholics Anonymous. It had been conceived a year or so before by two men, one a recovering alcoholic with many years of sobriety who knew depression first hand, and the other a former Catholic priest in the last difficult days of a marriage to a woman with a long history of unshakable depression. Both men understood the terribly destructive impact a depressed member can have on other family members. Together they decided to form a support group to help themselves and others who were in situations similar to theirs.

The first evening I attended, about thirty people had gathered in the dining room of an old restored mansion on Mission Street. A massive, handsome walnut table dominated the room. We pulled up chairs and gathered around it.

Before any introductions were made, I became aware of the presence of the former priest. He was a plain, small man, quiet, balding, in his sixties. Somehow, magically, he lit up the room. He seemed to be the spirit who led the way. Dressed almost shabbily in a loose brown sweater, there was an air about him such that clothes did not matter. I had a sense that this man might be a new saint Catholics had canonized, perhaps a St. Francis or a St. Augustine. His name was Armando. We used only first names at meetings.

After each of us had introduced ourselves, Armando addressed the group in an eloquent, professional manner: "All of us are here because we have a problem with co-dependency, a problem of how much help to give the depressive in our life. Our question is how to live with the sick person and still maintain our own boundaries, our own separateness. It's a fine balance we seek between acknowledging the diminished resources of the depressive and maintaining our own autonomy, insisting that they do something, *anything*, for themselves. Here in this room we help one another in the delicate task by drawing strength from one another, permitting ourselves the support of fellowship."

"Well spoken, little priest," I said to myself. "That's for me!"

Each of us was plagued with emotional problems, some larger than others, none small.

For a short while, sharing my sadness with the group afforded me some relief. At least I knew I was not alone in my pain. But as time wore on, week after week, I grew angrier each time I addressed the group, angry at having to go through a hell not of my own making. Soon I no longer wished to share. Soon I wished to avoid attending meetings. I faced each Monday night with a strange mixture of dread and anticipation. I no longer wished to speak of my misery—that was my dread. Yet I felt an overwhelming desire to see this charismatic leader, Armando—that was my anticipation. And so, when after each meeting he would quickly vanish out the door, I felt sadness. I would not see him for yet another week. But if I did not attend meetings I would not see him at all. I decided to share my dilemma with him. He had told us that he was a practicing psychotherapist. I could be open with him. He would certainly understand.

One night, following a meeting, I took Armando aside and, eyes cast down, embarrassed, I said quietly, "Armando, I'm not going to be coming anymore. It hurts too much to talk about my problem so many times, over and over. Truth be told, I'm coming now for only one reason, and that is to be near you, and that doesn't justify my coming, does it? I think I've fallen in love with you."

Armando looked dismayed. "I'm sorry," he said. "I was not aware of your feelings for me. Is there anything I did that led you to believe I had special feelings for you?"

"No," I answered. "You've done nothing. I seem to have fallen in love with the person I perceive you to be."

He spoke without guile. I heard the responsible, respectable monk in him speaking. He had been celibate until he was forty-seven, when he withdrew from the priesthood and married a woman with a long history of crippling depression. Optimistically, he wished to help her, but over the years, more and more, she closed down and withdrew from friends and all other resources. Now, sixteen years later, defeated, unable to cure or stem her illness, he was in the early months of filing for divorce. He had shared freely his anguish over this decision before the group, and now he worried that my feelings might be more compassion than love. I assured him this was not so.

Following our conversation I stopped attending the group. However, I did not stop seeing Armando. We began to meet, infrequently at first, then more often. Over time our relationship grew and blossomed. I am certain this was the prophecy portended by the magnificent Alaskan albatross; indeed, Armando represents the fulfillment of the divine promise of better things yet to be. When I am with Armando I am completely alive. Here is yet another of God's miracles! Serendipitously, in an unplanned, unexpected manner, a wonderful person had entered my life. I had sought surcease from sorrow, and by divine good fortune had found a supportive, beloved companion. Once again my heart began to sing.

Armando is a man who loves the world, a man who walks in God's way. He came to love me precisely as I am, though physically flawed. His acceptance helped me re-form and reconstruct the meaning of my life. He taught me to think of myself as beautiful, precisely as a woman, intelligent, capable, accomplished. And I no longer saw myself as I once had, a near-seventy-year-old woman with silver hair, a critical heart condition, two reconstructed hips, and shattered dreams. While he acknowledged the rude truth that I had been unfairly treated in life, he applauded my courage in having "hung in" despite major-league adversity and prejudice. He did not mock me or disapprove of my self-pity. His love created a miracle for me; I no longer saw myself through my own sad, myopic eyes, but rather through his optimistic hyperopic ones.

In addition, Armando has an impish sense of humor. He laughs easily, joyfully, and heartily, and I laugh with him. There is an old Buddhist saying: "He who learns to laugh laughs. He who learns to cry, cries." I had never before been taught to laugh, especially at myself, until Armando taught me how.

How very strange, even extraordinary, that the daughter of an Orthodox Jewish reverend steeped in Judaism and a former Catholic Franciscan monk steeped in Christianity could become so close in thought and love. This spiritual union could not have happened in our early years; it took difficult years of struggle and pain to bring us to the maturity and wisdom to accept one another and our differences unconditionally. While our pathways have certainly been different, we have miraculously broken through our religious barriers to arrive at the same moral high ground.

There is a beautiful song from the musical, *Barnum*, which precisely describes our union:

> *The colors of my life*
> *are bountiful and bold,*
> *the purple glow of indigo,*
> *the gleam of green and gold.*
> *The splendor of a sunrise,*
> *the dazzle of a flame,*
> *the glory of a rainbow,*
> *I'd put 'em all to shame.*
> *No quiet browns and grays,*
> *I'll take my days instead*
> *and fill them till they overflow*
> *with rose and cherry red.*
> *And should this sunlit world*
> *grow dark one day,*
> *the colors of my life*
> *will leave a shining light*
> *To show the way.*

Armando and I often had long, intense conversations about all manner of subjects. We talked about my overwhelming problems with Selina; about my failed twenty-three-year marriage; about my estranged daughter Sara, who had discarded me for reasons I did not understand; about my open-heart surgery and how I had come to the Pritikin Clinic only to remain and live in Santa Barbara; about how hurt I was at having been shunted to the outer circle of academia; and about my sense of failure as a woman, a mother, a wife, and especially as a scientist.

We talked about his former wife—her perpetual illnesses and her withdrawal from life; about the rigidity of the Catholic Church; about his political and religious rebellion in the '60s; about how he had come to study psychology after training with Dr. Carl Rogers at the Center for Studies of the Person in La Jolla; about how he had attended Catholic University in Washington, D.C., and, while studying there for a doctorate in canon law, realized that church law was based far more on the Roman Empire than on God; about the agony and the fear he felt on leaving the priesthood and the security of the Franciscan Brotherhood; and about the fulfilling psychotherapy he now practices with the poor and disenfranchised.

We talked about love and the divine, about God and spirituality, about reality and the supernatural, about sexuality and celibacy, about Christ and Moses and Buddha and Eli Weisel, about beautiful sunsets and the rush of the ocean, about the beauty of nature and God's hand in all of it, about the core of goodness in each person, about the miserable state of the homeless and starving uncared-for children, about art and music, and about the Holocaust and evil and good. In all our discussions we found no areas of serious incompatibility, no argument, no divisiveness. Together we decided we were good with one another.

I owe this man a great debt. It is he who has made all the difference in my life. It is he who cheered me on to write the book I had been talking and dreaming about for many years.

"For once," he said, "take something from life which you truly want. You have felt the need to write your story. Do it now! Send your message! Tell the world what it has done to women who have aspired to something other than domesticity, who have attempted to crash the sacred male enclave and have been brutally driven back. You still have time to vindicate yourself. Speak out for humanity's sake, if not alone for your own."

While Selina still remains a large part of my life today, I have learned to set limits on her access to me. She no longer completely invades my life and home as she once did. And she has survived. In fact she has grown stronger for it. As I push on with my new-found love, I feel I can face whatever life presents, even as the shadow of years descends upon us both.

Conclusion—De Profundis _____

Glory to those who hope
For freedom is theirs
Those who stand unflinching
against the mountain
Shall gain its summit.

I will never deny my bitter experience of rejection and disparagement at the hands of the male academic powers. It was truly a grave injustice they dealt my dreams, dreams I had cherished and held close to my heart from childhood. My dreams had grown to define me, to crowd out all else from my life. When it became clear to me that my academic goals could never be achieved, I was left with no substantial identity. For many years I remained in a wounded position, intimidated, weak, cowering, awaiting yet the next blow. That was the case as long as I remained married to Bud.

Following my divorce I permitted myself to grieve, to relive my angst. I stormed against my life full of seeming failure. When finally the dust settled, I carefully examined the rubble. It was true. My academic dreams were indeed shattered. My long marriage had failed. My roles as wife and mother were cancelled. In my final disappointment I might have surrendered my will to live. Instead, with Armando's help, I surrendered to a Wisdom greater than my own, relaxed my death grip on an elusive career and, thus energized, began to move forward toward personal fulfillment.

I could finally see clearly what my life meant. For the first time I understood that I had mistakenly defined myself in the world primarily as a scientist, then, in defeat, frustration, and desperation, as a wife and as a mother. But never once had I considered myself a worthy person. With Armando's help I was able to peer beneath the surface of my overburdened ego. There I discovered my God-given Self with a mine of opportunities in a place of abundance. There I found also the magnificent jewels of my womanliness—my intelligence, my grace. I learned how to accept love and how to provide unconditional love to others. I finally discovered my unique place in the universe even as a woman—especially as a woman. Had I achieved success, it is possible I might never have been able to write this story. My failed academic dream might never have been transformed into the reality of a book which would tell people the story of a woman's bitter exclusion from what she most desired from life—to be recognized as a scientist, with equal rights and privileges granted to male scientists—and what unhappiness ensued as a consequence of this exclusion.

From birth, my family, society, and even my religion had taught me that women were always to assume a subordinate role to men. Now, almost too late, I have found my voice. "No fair!" I cry out. This thinking has reserved first place for men throughout the ages, while we women followed six steps behind. I am no longer content to stay six steps behind.

As I listen to the drumbeat of the current women's movement, I hear accompanying it a shrill voice stridently demanding acceptance and recognition. It is not a soft, mellifluous, feminine voice. It is not a harmonious, lyrical voice. It is, rather, the militant voice of revolution, a justifiably angry equal rights voice, a voice of war—women's war against men. At times it sounds hostile, violent, threatening. On hearing it, I know that most men must cringe. Some men must be angered. Some must fall back in fear. But all men must, in their collective conscious or unconscious, be aware that they have oppressed women mightily. As a result of male domination, many women through the centuries have lived lives of quiet desperation, dissatisfied, frustrated, and unfulfilled. As have I. Our unhappiness has rubbed off on all those close to us, on the very men who have denied us and on the children we have borne those same men. The choice of what to do with our lives was not ours to make. I am not a revolutionist; I do not propose war against men. I am, rather, an evolutionist. I know that, given time, equality will ultimately prevail. The long-held myth that men are superior, stronger, and more creative than women will certainly be set aside as both genders surrender to the reality that their destinies are inextricably intertwined.

Each day, now that I have found my Self, I live life to the fullest. I smell the rose and revel in its divine perfection. I glory in the color of the sky as the sun sets and paints pinks and mauves across the face of heaven. I stand in awe atop the majestic mountain, and I have no fear as I gaze down upon the panorama of my life. Now, with only a little time left to me on earth, but with a strength I have developed from years of doggedly searching for my place in the world, I am satisfied. I have but one remaining wish. Gently, ever so gently, so as to harm no one, seeking only to do good, I wish to slam the door on all bigots of whatever gender, on all prejudice of whatever kind, on all inequity wherever it exists.

Seventy-odd years ago, when I was young, equality and acceptance of women was nowhere to be found, not even on the far distant horizon. But today, I feel the still, small stirrings of change. Slowly, gradually, one tiny step at a time, women are being accepted as persons worthy of responsibility in service jobs outside the home. Opportunities in places once totally barred to them are beginning to appear, unlikely places like outer space, the ocean's depth, the Supreme Court, the military, and even the science departments of universities. It behooves us women to seize this day, to expand this day—not with rancor, not with anger, but with gentle, unyielding firmness. As it says in the Book of Proverbs: "She openeth her mouth with wisdom, kindness is on her tongue. Strength and dignity are her clothing; and she laugheth at the time to come." (Prov. 31)

On the Day of Atonement, as the sun begins to set, Jews throughout the world begin to chant the final prayer of the High Holy Days, the *N'eela*. The old year is fast coming to a close. Cleansed and refreshed, at the end of an arduous soul-searching day of fasting and prayer, I look forward to leaving the temple to face a new year. Each Yom Kippur I feel a surge of emotion as the day begins to fade. As I lift my eyes from the prayerbook to see the sun sinking below the horizon, I importune God in the final prayer of this most holy day: "Open to us, O God, the Gates of Mercy, before the closing of the gates, ere the day is done. The day vanishes. The sun is setting. Let us hurry to enter Thy gates."

AUTHOR'S ARTICLES IN SCIENTIFIC JOURNALS

"The Anatomical Effects of Air Pollution on Plants," *Proceedings of the Second Air Pollution Symposium*, Stanford Research Institute, 1952, pp. 129–133.

"The Effect of Smog on the Anatomy of Oat Leaves," *Phytopathology*, 1952, Vol. 42, pp. 558–563.

"Use of Plants as Biological Indicators of Smog in the Air of Los Angeles County," *Science* 12, #1245, 1955, pp. 510–511.

"The Leaf Structure of *Poa annua* with Observations on Its Smog Sensitivity in Los Angeles County," *American Journal of Botany*, Vol. 42, #5, May, 1955, pp. 467–474.

"Cork Formation in Table Beet (*Beta vulgaris*) in Response to Smog," *Proceedings of the Third National Air Pollution Symposium*, Stanford Research Institute, 1955, pp. 199–206.

"Smog Damage to Ferns in the Los Angeles Area," *Phytopathology*, vol. 46, #12, December 1956, pp. 696–698.

"A Developmental Study of the Leaves of *Nicotiana glutinosa* as Related to Their Smog Sensitivity in Los Angeles County," R.A. Bobrov Glater, Richard A. Solberg and Flora M. Scott, *American Journal of Botany*, vol. 49, #9, October 1962, pp. 954–970.

"Electron Microscope Study of Epidermal Tissue of *Beta vulgaris* Subjected to Los Angeles Type Air Pollution," R.A. Bobrov Glater, Barbara Bystrom and Edward Bowler, *Botanical Gazette*, vol. 129, #2, June 1968, pp. 133–135.

"Appraisal of Manifestation of Plant Damage in Response to Air Pollutants," report written for Systems Development Corporation, Santa Monica, California, 1969.

"Lead Detection in Living Plant Tissue Using a New Histochemical Method," R.A. Bobrov Glater and Louis Hernandez, Jr., *Air Pollution Control Association Journal*, vol 22, #6, June 1972, pp. 463–467.

RECOMMENDED READING

Cole, Jonathan R., *Fair Science: Women in the Scientific Community* (New York: Columbia University Press, 1987).

Friedan, Betty, *The Feminine Mystique* (New York: W.W. Norton & Co., 1963).

Frommer, Myrna & Harvey, *It Happened in the Catskills* (New York: Harcourt Brace Jovanovich, 1991).

Grotjahn, Martin, *Beyond Laughter* (New York: McGraw Hill, 1957).

Gunther, John, *Roosevelt in Retrospect* (New York: Harper and Bros., 1950).

Heschel, Abraham Joshua, *The Earth is the Lord's* (New York: Henry Schuman, 1950. Reprinted by Jewish Lights Publishing, Woodstock, Vermont, 1955).

Howe, Irving, *World of Our Fathers* (New York: Simon and Schuster, 1976).

Keller, Evelyn Fox, *A Feeling for the Organism* (New York: W.H. Freeman Co., 1983).

Kerber, Linda K., and De Hart, Jane Sherrow, *Women's America: Refocusing the Past*. (New York; Oxford University Press, 1991.)

Lacey, Robert, *Little Man: Meyer Lansky and the Ganster Life* (Boston: Little, Brown and Co., 1991).

Lipset, Seymour, and Ladd, Carl, *Jewish Academics in the U.S.: Their Achievements, Culture & Politcs* (New York: American Jewish Year Book, 1971–1972; Jewish Publication Society of America, 1972).

Marcus, Jacob Rader, *United States Jewry, 1776–1985* (Indiana: Wayne State University, 1989).

Novick, Peter, *That Noble Dream* (Cambridge: Cambridge University Press, 1988).

Rossiter, Margaret W., *Women Scientists in America* (Baltimore, Johns Hopkins University Press, 1983).

Rosten, Leo, *The Joys of Yiddish* (New York: Pocket Books, 1970).

Yeager, William A., *Adminstration and the Teacher* (New York: Harper and Bros., 1954).